'*Disquiet Drive* is restless ...esse κ's writing vibrates with the quiet solar intensity of a planetary body that can't be looked at directly: things slip, slink, snick and lick into each other, limning a gorgeous periphery where genre, past and future selves, follies, fossils and hormones collide. I can't remember when I last read something as exhilarating, beautiful and deeply attuned to the implications and contradictions involved in struggling towards a bearable world, and the 'undomesticated sensibility' it requires of us.'

~ DAISY LAFARGE

'Buck wild and entirely unique, *Disquiet Drive* took me to the beautiful and chaotic edge of the universe and made me want to write (live) for 200 years.'

~ ELIOT DUNCAN

baby   i'd split my shell   for y ou

but still the world   is   what   it is cut u p in   to

DISQUIET DRIVE

Hesse K.

For

D, M, O, F, D, M, H, J & G

This book lives at the limit edge of the body
and/in
the first flush of language.

In sitting down to start, I realised that it had been
being written for a long time,

not by me.

1~

SPILLDOZER

A stumbling game of pool took place on the only table left lit from above, adrift in the cavernous dark. All the lights in the whole building were out. Floors and floors of indifference. Balls, clacking against one another before firming into shape, moved like constellations: their patterns looked stable only from the vantage of the centre. Ursa Minor snicked apart, squeezed between damp crinoline, warm beer and black leather chaps. Orion straddled the green firmament before pausing. In the glint of his eye and the surety of his dominance we both perceived a judgement, and scrambled to break him apart into something diffuse again, like silica. Dim flies pestered the single bulb guttering over the table while brown bottles piled up like cartridges, spent. There was an irregular dripping noise. If you sit under a flightpath for long enough you will be able to count the pulse of your heart in time with the long doppler of a private jet. Its trails are reinscribing money, or the power to traverse. Somewhere a bird flags. Somewhere two seals crest black water through soft ribbons of sea-ice, like tulle. A woman is followed home, she reaches for her phone. Then: heel on the edge of the table, sweltering thigh in the skew of an L, blue chalked cue bowing across the whole arrangement like sheet music. The toilets flood again and we splash toward the door through the cold inch of anguish that hovers over the linoleum. I don't know really. Basically I am just here. Planes pour over me.

As a child, light flickered across the window in streaks. Against the odds I rarely felt the need for other people, but in the collapse of a book I stayed with where I'd been.

Our house was built only a mile or so from the cliff edge, so from an early age I knew where it all ended. How the land gave out. Words as speech held little promise, but in being sentenced to the page they accrued; built an image.

Images made a knowing.
Knowing made a kind of animal.

Under the house was a maze of crawl-space. Smelled of dank soil. Wet granite. I traversed it in the night. Things were laid flat at first but then they stood on their side. Becoming implicit. Snowdrops in February, bluebells in spring. Things had a habit of slipping here — of breaking into other things, smaller ruins. Flint to wash, bracken to tinder, cinder to spit: always the sea. Then it all slipped into chiffony, something diaphanous.

One winter a stag crossed our path in the deep snow.

Growing came on quickly. Thick bands of pale skin opened up at the base of my spine like snakes through milk. They found I had poor eyesight. Corrected, I watched a tree move in the wind for the first time. My silhouette was loose, tentatively goth.

Letters took on a kind of gauze. At first they shuffled along like a string of condemned men and let out barky derives. Then they closed their trunk to me as clover at dusk.

> 'I ran into the world of books, the only living world I, a girl, could find'.[1]

> 'It is girls from which stories begin'.[2]

Slowly meaning was pried open, but in the prying its shape grimaced and jagged. Slim fingers ran along its saw-toothed edge, very softly. *My body needed to find a way to live.*

One afternoon I woke to discover that I had become indivisible from a ruin which was fake. A fake ruin which dwindled on the edge of that cliff. At first I thought it was an armature upon which to gibbet the wet clay of my pronoun, but now I understand that it was in fact a crucible at the very lip of gender.

Much later, I arrived at the house of a lover and found a fox sleeping under immaculate bushes of sage. Mostly I worked. I worked in kitchens and on roads and in offices which neither I nor anyone else occupied. Soon I would learn that I was tinged with regret and that I was pursuing an envelope; some new folding or permutation and the tacky adhesion to a limit. I had been an object of mediation or, more accurately, a performance — and so ground it's nightly slink down like an eyeglass.

Every morning I would cycle along the edge of a four lane motorway leading out of a medium-sized city in the hour before dawn, intermittently flushed on my left side by the steady thrum of headlights in step. I saw no one. This was in 2017. Cleaved by the early morning traffic two equal halves of the city stretched out on either side of me. Scurrying along the tract of its thickest artery, I failed to realise that I was softly cupped by the daily becoming of being a commuter. I failed to realise many things. I was neither alone nor entirely aware of communing in this journey with millions. At work I would talk to Hussein, Hussein who was Maasai; who had taught young men to blink-sleep, rifle clutched, to protect corrals of sheep. Hussein who had a tattoo of a bald eagle splayed across his chest with an enormous throbbing cock which I heard about but never saw. Mostly we talked about his insomnia. Now he mixed dried fruit and grains.

It's necessary to lose almost everything in every attempt at expression. I lost a lot through misdirection. Most of what I lost was time.

Satellites *twizt*

as

they fall

out ,

of

the

sky.

And then, without voice; a crash.

Last week she came off her bike, straight over the handlebars, and mewled in the street cowling about a broken thumbnail. Her intended destination further up the hill — the pub — spat at a narrow threshold of plausibility before guttering out.

She lay there for a minute or so, undisturbed. It was a quiet street.

Some saw, perhaps others didn't, but the occasional cyclists that followed behind carved a wide arc around her foetal repose. Apprehending bliss, they kept a wide berth.

Directly opposite the crash was a lurid yellow wood panelled garage door with the Ferrari, Lamborghini and Abarth insignias arranged in a blazing triptych above the entranceway. She knew this door well. A few years ago she'd had time to kill, like everyone had, and peered closer to discover that its ironwork hinges, bolted to the wood and inlaid in sprawling patterns, were actually painted on, not forged. Each line had the gestural lick of the calligrapher. She lay there and felt her hip swell quietly and watched that door horizontally, hoping for the slightest twitch — the clean rev and mangle of black pistons before a violent outward splintering. A rupture in retiree manicure.

Slowly the blood cloyed in the ruffles of her skirt and she breathed deep into the green tarmac.

This is a genre which simply appears.

Where she picked gravel from her palm in the sink, scrubbing diligently with slugs of peachy foam, a scab the texture of canvas unfurled like a picnic blanket. The surface of the scab is livid, which makes it hard to type. Also my E is loose. This is a point of weakness in the script. Occasionally the pad of my left index finger, whether because it is oily, or puckered at the right angle, will excise the E clean out from the board to skitter down and across past S and D, to X.

Between the wilful E and the itch of a scab something other than ten fingers and this beleaguered machine must be attended to. Someone's said it before. Writing asks for many pauses. To write and then stop and then read before craning to write again. And also to write in the full, dependable glee of drilling out. Redolently you re-enter:

There were small black mushrooms like dried ears encircling the bough where it wove its way into the trunk. We picked them auspiciously for eventual rehydration. Large bulls were avoided, veering instead onto a too green-golf course, before realising — as we got back to the car — that highland cattle always have horns. Below, a brook reluctantly let go of itself to spill in the hollow of a mire.

'Things happen indirectly. They come sideways'.[3]

Later, we would take blood in a vial in a bag and place it inside a red plastic box inside another bag slung onto our backs, and sign our initials and the precise minute of collection in a large diary to indicate that the blood had been taken. Sometimes it was not blood, but piss. Or oncology medicine in thick, leaded yellow wallets. Very occasionally, shit — which would rattle softly in the tube. The rasping biro which we used to score our initials into the diary was strung to its spine by a ribbon of folded tape. Each week, without fail, it would give out before the week was done.

When I say 'we' I mean that there were several of us. A grim troupe. Dishevelled and wiry, we retained an air of plausible deniability. It clung to us each like a fog. Vagrancy and all that came with it — hyper-visibility, impalpability, disavowal — silvery miasmas; we wore them each like a buffer, or a boon. Together but alone, employed and yet not, we lingered in ostentatious waiting rooms while our T-shirts grew large holes.

Sweat eventually takes on the quality of bleach.

Some of us wrote poems there, whilst waiting. They had to be short. Twelve minutes were all the time we had before the next collection would be ready, and so each poem became dense, lateral, bitten-off.

If a sentence is allowed to sit around for too long without amendment it will retreat into itself, becoming impossible to retrieve. There's now nothing new to refine. The only edits left to make are panoramic, surgical ones.

London and Glasgow, then London again. Marseille, Derbyshire, Devon. Santa Fe. Pluck back the eyelid of any given year at all and peer under the hood, its premise. You never know what you might let in. That's why she listens out for words on the train like *acerbic* or *mint*. And watches for the murmur of a reader's lips as they mouth their sentences noiselessly, eyes glazing.

Really there are more important things to regret but a large part of me wishes that *sick* had made its way into my vocabulary; passed from you through trenchant osmosis. Occasionally I'll try it out in conversation but of course think of you immediately, revealing in that failed attempt at mimicry that this is a false doubling, not a sapphic one.

The summer before last the upstairs neighbours moved out, tore their washing machine from the wall, and forgot to turn the mains off. She came back from Scotland to a brown nimbus hovering above the bed, dripping nonchalant into the sheets. It was the colour of something over-brewed: the steeping pitch at which that nacreous, silvery scum sticks into brittle archipelagos that play Pangea on the surface.

Moving becomes much easier once you internalise the logic that anything can be thrown away.

'Fingernails are supposed to be the endings of the sun's rays'.[4]

Evidently I want to transform in such a way that no one can lay claim to me. Not to 'exceed myself' in the sense that I die or cease to be known — in thin slices — as what I've always appeared to have been, but rather that

I want to reach escape velocity. This isn't a wish to leave those problems of contact behind; problems of memory; partners; ex-partners or lovers; of family, institutions, communities, scenes; responsibilities toward others and duties to yourself; rent due; promises rescinded; projects wilted; shifts to attend — but rather to change so utterly that such problems can no longer find purchase in your body. Until they brush flaccid against the strange walls of new permissions. Again, it is not that you have died but have simply been ambiguated.

To re-emerge as a blinding pinprick of light, un-made in an apotheosis of autonomy, is in its own way to become a kind of alien. To be ontologically ungraspable. Finally it becomes possible to think about the future but the past, in all its language, is held in abeyance. A small cottage outside Toulouse or somewhere. Long wheat, a doe in the bracken, solitude. Simply you were that, and now you are something else.

This might read as an admission of loneliness because it is. Compressed to the point of obsolescence, are these old problems of association really problems of proximity? Proximity to the threshold of being perceived, or to the possibility of exchange? Really here we are talking about vulnerability, or of having a body altogether.

Unfurl too frequently and the cornflower loses its hue.

Often I am licked down by an absolute blankness in the brain. Then things start surging on their own. In that scourge of activity I understand that my body is furious from being compressed like a spider. All afternoon I'll wander around aimlessly until some other sentence lurches into my head. There is a deep well here, and I can never quite seem to draw water from it.

London again, closer to the river this time. Stepping back once more over the barren rut of the slurbs she watched the whole abrupt bloat lilt back and forth from the top of the hill behind the old house, the old house that's new again, new now for the third time. The city was cast a deep orange by smog, pollen. Its blaze unspooled from the very low sky to comb through undulate grass. And then the rain came; fast and warm.

Picking her way across a meadow in the mountains of Bulgaria she first realised what had already been lost, as a limitless chorus of insects detonated into the air with every step. This was the reminder that we are supposed to be absolutely adrift in everything else.

You are, or have always been, the pistil of the rose.

A feeling of wanting or of trying to write only gets more urgent, but the gaps between sittings distend. You hear about someone in Croydon who is making poems with light and shadow. They are durational, and yawn across the studio at different times of day.

Writing is the reminder that you want to live, irredeemably. This isn't a decision, more the fulcrum your body offers. The mind can go anywhere but the body only bends so far.

That second night there we drove up to the mesa behind the house, picked our way across a steely mesh where concrete was to be poured, drank whiskey, and listened to coyotes whooping in the brightest dark.

'5. This note is written across a dance program (c. 1967) and it is not entirely clear whether it refers to a "girl" being an object or a sculptor.'

~ Lucy Lippard[5]

~GENEROSITY AND ITS SISTERS

Ralph Waldo Emerson once wrote that language is fossil poetry. He might have meant many things by that, but here are some of them:

i)   Below the current usage of a word lies a bedrock of lost and archaic metaphor.

ii)   Language is built, always and in real time, upon a beach of calcified tongues.

iii)   Bones of old associations accrue in the soil just as 'the limestone of the continent consists of infinite masses of the shells of animalcules'.

iv)   Behind the expression of a single word there persists that which is plural, and far older, than the word itself.

v)   Behind the accretion of metaphor there persists something singular, and more violent, than the images themselves.

vi)   Metaphors have a habit of proliferating.

vii)   They are generous.

viii)   You must resist the urge to make meaning.

viiii)   You must let both your language and your body swim in the peal.

x)   A fossil, like a skeleton, is what is left behind.

Is a fossil *behind* the body of which it was once part? Or is it already behind the compacted mud and rock which it is found embedded in?

I read an article about a type of fossilised moss that had been exhumed by archeologists. The moss, when it was alive, had grown into the cuneiform grooves of a limestone slab engraved with the name of the moss, and died there.

By blooming a lexical body, the moss had become both sign, signifier and signified. The name of the plant prefigured its own physical existence, and so became a reality in and of itself. The moss had grown into its own name.

The archeological community were, it's fair to say, underwhelmed. They understood the moss-name as an entirely predictable phenomena brought about by dependably random variables in heat, pressure and moisture. Given what they understood of the local geological record (which was little) and the cultural history of the society that had engraved the cuneiform (which was prejudiced), they felt safe in ruling out any possibility of intentionality on the part of both the local culture, or the moss.

The loose-knit towns and villages which made up the local community rejected this premise. Although there were naysayers and disinterested parties amongst them, generally they held the same opinion as their parents before them: it was only natural — even inevitable — that the moss would prosper best in the site most suited to it. Some even argued that the engraving of the name and the growth of the moss were desynchronous, and that the scoring of the cuneiform had actually invoked the plant's coming into the world.

At the true fringe of the debate, and of society, an even smaller group insisted that the cuneiform predated any record of human activity in the area. They argued that the engraving was not the work of human hands, but instead had simply needed to be — and so became. The moss was, to their mind, ancillary to the 'real', unauthored work of the etching itself, which had been scored in the rock instantaneously, as one of nature's many flourishes. Their words gained some traction, but converted few, both because they were obdurate, and because they couldn't explain where the cuneiform had come from.

And, as is always the case, in the backlit rooms of dark houses with winding corridors, fuming with dank candles and the reek of tallow, old women swaddled in rags croaked out their sureties. They intoned that every twenty-seven years, on the last moon of winter as worms turned the earth, if the correct rights had been performed and with no small amount of luck, the moss-name would flower. Its flowers were so minute that bees could barely brush against them to collect their bright pollen — being as they were insubstantial, like stars.

> 'There are names under things and names inside names'.[6]

In truth the plant is fictional. It was used by the author of the article as a metaphor for a new kind of parallel typography they were developing.

But

> 'An intent is just as material as the thing pursued, or the thing pursuing'.[7]

And

'The shortest poem is a name'.[8]

Like

"*Rimbaud* is spelled with seven letters of the
alphabet [...] with seven passages
A E I O U Y
And that stony vowel called death".[9]

The final, hidden secret of the world is that you can
speak it.

~YOUR DRESS SAYS EASY TARGET

I begin re-reading *Un Captif Amoureux* and someone calls it a memoir that is a bomb. I walk to B&Q with you and feel my language leaking out of me: it is ensconced in the cold drive to put my body on the line.

Things are so far gone and the goalposts have moved so utterly that it's easy to believe people can no longer say things with their full throat. There is false-nuance and there is generalised antipathy and there is pausing in McDonald's, watching a line cook who can't be older than sixteen, and remembering your own first gauntlet of shift work, its depersonalisation.

I come back to Genet for a lot of things. For starting again and for looking long. For invoking what Edward Said called 'an utterly undomesticated sensibility',[10] and it's this sensibility which I reinscribe repeatedly into my body as I read, because it is a gesture toward decolonisation. In that reading I again begin the shedding of good sense, respectability, moral relativism, civility, deference, all conformities; of gender and thiefdom; carceral logics and hierarchies of violence, apologia, bourgeois syntax; arbitrary distances. All that separates you from anyone else is a splinter in the thumb.

Like everyone in a very particular circle I read the Fred Moten quote, "I just need you to realise that this shit is killing you, too, however much more softly, you stupid motherfucker, you know?" and remember, with guilt, that I have grown a crust to survive, like shellac, like always, and that this crust is antithetical to a politics of coalition. It's a long brindled slug of a scab and it yawns open with new picking, but better — always — to be inflamed and tingling. Because guilt without action is worse than apathy, and unforgivably inert. Really the choices are: spiral into a mire of complicity or hack a wedge out of yourself. Nothing else matters but the hinge of an arm.

In a throng of three hundred thousand people I begin crying uncontrollably. You both wait for me and we begin walking together, solemn at first. Like you can't catch the breath in your throat. Soon downpour and haze fill the street to its brim while the Met's helicopters squat over everything, like ticks on a lens. They've come to feed. Or just harvest faces. How far away can you pick us out from? Can you triangulate the snarl of a lip, hooded eyes, a grimace? Do my streaming tears help identify me? I cry in public a lot.

Yes you fucker I know you're on top, don't worry.

I've covered my face but feel it boring into me all the same. That impossible scrutiny and latent militance. True anonymity is unworkable, and as a deviant woman I strive for it, but still under its gaze I'm made naked, and so begin shedding all of it, suddenly: the ossification, the rain, the grief as it accretes, the chronic poison of my phone and everything steeled since 2019. My body, deemed deviant, that Genet shores up; the deemed deviance of a people fleeing genocide that Genet dwelled within, for all that time. Who marked us both for death?

This might sound trite but I mean it with the deepest feeling: it's not reductive to be rocked by a sudden and seamless awareness of the world's indivisible violence, as it is writ upon you and upon everyone else. Genet lived his life knotting it all together — tracing the interstices, running his fingers over each aperture. The wounds. There are no separate struggles for liberation, that's the lesson of vagrancy; what being criminalised teaches you.

Fascism, we know, has no logic and so it cannot be unmade by logic. Only by feeling. By which I mean that I'm glad that you're here with me, walking, at this threshold where language begins to break down, numbed by the violence of a thousand vertices, before swelling again in unison. By which I mean, I am grateful not just for you but for our *we*. Together, here on the street. Together at the same moment that your deviant body is being offered the chance to begin again, just as mine has, and so we hide it, under our clothes — from the police and from our comrades today and under the blank eye of the helicopters.

We are not wired to comprehend this but we have to try. Fascism resists language because it destroys meaning, but nothing is beyond expression. That was another lesson you taught me.

If we are all only writing about our inability to write, if we are able to write only about transfixion, paralysis, then really we deserve to write nothing at all. There's the tip of the spear and then there's this. There's lingering and there's being backed into a corner and then there's this. The page. The page which is empty, or filled only by words which allude to an inarticulable horror — which might as well be a sea of guilt; thick and indulgent.

Chris Kraus said Simone Weil was wracked by a 'panic of altruism', which we might read as a grappling with her own complicity; the relative comfort of her class. When I think of Weil, I can't shake the image of her squinting short-sighted down the irons of a rifle, shoulder-to-breast with the Durutti Column, taking aim at one of Franco's bombers: the blazing sun glints off the barrel, she fumbles the trigger, and misses. Later she would burn herself on a cooking fire and be asked to leave. Her parents had to come and collect her.

This vision of Weil's incompetence is clearly some kind of internalised misogyny, or rather the incorrect assumption that she was a revolutionary of the mind only, because she continually threw her meagre body against danger, over and over, even in hunger and voluntary repatriation, after her mother and father had fled to America. But still what she sought was sacrifice, not death. To use her body as a tool.

Simone, born with everything, sought poverty out, its every permutation, in rapture. Not quite a comrade but something more expiatory. Genet, born with nothing, accepted invitations from struggles for liberation across the globe. No longer a convict but something more fugitive. Like Weil we have to tease out our own inadequacy to dispense with it. Like Genet we have to know our own contradictions to go beyond them. This isn't a shedding of your own positionality, I'm not even sure that's useful. Simply that we have to begin with our own grief.

Feel some animal noise creak out of her body after lying in a coil for six hours on the floor

The first thing you do in the morning is stretch and listen out for the grinding squeal of the bin lorry as it disappears what's been piling up in the street

Try to feel out the soft edges of the mould your shape slept in

I have my hands down my pants and read a letter to the editor from a 1992 issue of FTM Newsletter in which the correspondent describes our collective experience as one of "going both directions"

C and I once spoke about coming out to writing first

They described themselves as "travelling-through"

Train up north to get estrogen

There's a fire on the tracks, everything overground is cancelled

London Bridge instead, then down underground

The heat of the carriage is like a hex; there's nothing else to say about it

Tropical juice and anaemic coconut from a transparent punnet

Up on the surface kids ride motorbikes in vests and silver shorts that reflect the light

Three guys in blacked-out crash helmets on delimited Segways do forty — they mount the pavement at points

The road is all theirs

So is her gaze

She realises that it's summer

On the street people know they look good; try to strut

having fully internalised that knowledge

Everyone begins to break down at the edges but also

takes on an incredible clarity

People hit her like trains

Across the road, there's an international transfer place

under a big white awning with a queue of people

outside, and next door, under the same awning, a

restaurant filled with more people, grey steam and

curling laughter

Both the transfer place and the restaurant share a long

brown counter upon which employees lean, across

which cards and cash are exchanged

Funds abroad, fried food aside

I realise I want to write as if I were driving across

America; as if I made photographs or films

But I can't, and don't

Hope in the heart it's not voyeurism — just a symptom

of condensing

Wait around for hours

You had a loose plan to meet but not a confirmed one

Coming up here was a gesture of faith, you're not sure

in what; if it happens it does

All you can do is hold your hand out the window of a

moving car and take what comes

It's one of the few ways to make the air feel material

She kills time with her phone bluntly, as if disinterested

There's a coquettish brutality at work in the ease at which she'll offer up an hour

Put it on the block

It could be said that her demeanour is like a Morning Star

While waiting she avoids groups of men who linger and smoke

Whose lingering — unlike hers — has the texture of leisure, not apprehension

But who inevitably she can't help but read through a thin film of threat

Capricious onlooking gets sharply curbed at the gnarled edge of a stare

Or rather:

Something gnawed long and then erupted

Forget to eat

Know the cramps will come on soon if you don't

On the way back south, empty-handed, the tube is completely uninhabited

Not just the carriage you boarded, but both carriages adjacent to you, too

This is unprecedented

Everything rocks furiously side to side but your body, only your body alone, is jostled in the rocking

She hangs off the support bars and stares down the aisle through both sets of adjoining windows to feel the snake of it all under the earth:

watching the curvature of the tunnel as it devours the nose of the train

This perspective allows her to see the shape of its route through the dark where usually there's no visual reference

It is very eerie

She feels dizzy, and wonders if she might have lost consciousness — but realises that she needs to piss excruciatingly, which reassures her that she is indeed awake

Still, it's blindingly hot

In places the caustic heat has unstuck the textured linoleum from the centre of the carriage

It swells in little mounds like miniature diagrams of a megalithic earthwork

Grief has its own abraded lilt

We each share words that are in time intoned by the budding mouth of a moan

I've been taught to understand the grief of a community as a substance auratic and flat

These lessons have been largely elliptical:

A walk in the New Forest that never came to an end

A fall from scaffolding

Climbing the roof of a hotel in Paris to look at the full moon

Digging the grave of a dog in a snowstorm

He hadn't eaten in a month

A Glaswegian guy in a jockey's cap on the way to visit his mum in the hospital told me *they don't make shrouds with pockets*

I used to suppress everything I could because it's not enough to say that these four things are the same

Do you remember the way you would rock side to side and feel your kidneys flare hot, because you were holding in a hot piss, playing *Final Fantasy* in 2003?

In that feverish stalling of a need we might be able to dredge up other negations

Like how you absently turn a lozenge of soap over and over in your armpit while washing, as if you're polishing something venerated

Or the car keys to the white Fastback with the tarnished plastic Snowy rocking soporific in the ignition as you sank as deeply as possible into your seat; mortified by waiting in a distinctive car in a village of three thousand people while your mum went to the shops for fear of being any type of known

What of it?

There is a way of crying in the presence of someone else that is shallow and long enough that it can simply end, and you will stand up and run a scalding hot bath and nothing else need be said on the matter

Standing at Whitechapel station the week before you both watched a fox cub skittering down the edge of the track, hugging the wall

It was completely black, had no tail, and padded out a

faint da-dum da-dum as it ran

How long had it been down there?

The cub had the broken look of something that has never stopped running, and never would; tracing an endless circuit underneath the river and back again

There are people who live quietly underground, in decommissioned subway tunnels, like these

They've built houses, a high street

They smoke and argue and love each other before bustling about under the harsh light of day

Their various routes home are cramped, scattered about, or completely arcane

Some have garbage cans placed over them

Some are under bridges

And then there's Eric, the messenger

When he's really down and out he walks straight off the end of the platform and sleeps in a maintenance cupboard with 27,000 volts overhead

At dawn he climbs straight out from the grate to the street

He's already at the end of his wick, you can see it

It flares in the crook of his grin when he speaks about his daughter

The grooves in the lino on the floor of the carriage contour over the mounds and intersect, giving them the texture of keratin

Animal armour

She thinks of Scott Walker and the crust she's growing

to survive

And toys with going for a piss in the corner of the carriage

When asked, you once heard John say "writing returns my experience to me"

It was a trite answer to a trite question so you never found out whether what was returned to him was a gift or a kind of ballast

We make our own language, really

We make it because we need it

It's not that we are special, but that we are each made from something extra[11]

That night Grant showed us how to look at the sunset as if from above

By letting your eyes slip out of focus slightly, the clouds nearest the horizon become the shoreline, the sky becomes the sea

The sun remains the sun

But winks into the sky which is the ocean now

And it all dips slowly

Samuel Delaney's *Heavenly Breakfast*, his short memoir of a single winter living in a commune in New York's East Village between 1967-68, begins:

> *This book is dedicated*
> *to everyone who ever*
> *did anything*
> *no matter how sane or crazy*
> *whether it worked out or not*
> *to give themselves*
> *a better life.*

Mum says every time she goes back to the town where I grew up and she entered middle-age — where she spent the best part of twenty years — it gets worse and worse. It was bad enough in the aughts. Most of the shop fronts are boarded up now, she says, in flaking plywood or those seemingly mandatory, gestural daubs that get streaked across the windows when a place goes belly up. Like they need to block out the failure. Then she hangs up. All the friends who died here; all the friends who didn't leave. That gangly kid Josh who used to half-live at mine and the pale smileys on his arms where his dad put fags out on him. His gran used to play poker online. People work so furiously hard to justify their own aspirationalism to themselves — all the writing and back-bending, the semantics. One night we were up late looking at their painting of an orange house with *GRASS* scrawled over the brickwork in big white letters and D let slip: "people will do anything but just be working class".

Heavenly Breakfast is the name of the book, the band, and the commune in which all of the members of the band — including Delaney — lived. The Breakfast had three rooms: the main room, which included a kitchen, freestanding bath and toilet, and two smaller rooms used exclusively for recording music and selling weed out of. At any one time there was between ten to fifteen residents of The Breakfast, alongside a revolving cast of friends, visitors, collaborators and strays; their children or friends. The Breakfast apparently 'never had anything close to resembling an organisational meeting' and, at one point, when quizzed about how much they paid in rent, Delaney can't decide 'whether to divide seventy-five dollars a month by ten, twelve or fifteen'. Some passages from this book slip into feeling like scenes from his 1975 science fiction epic *Dhalgren* — the orgies and group meals, the arguments. Like *Times Square Red, Times Square Blue* the feverish bohemia of late sixties and early seventies New York that Delaney describes feels so impossibly distant it might as well be a piece of sci-fi itself: the total permeation of erotics into urban space, the rent. I read these books and think *oh — this is what they took from us.*

It's hard for me to say why I left the town I grew up in. I didn't really think about it at the time. I knew I wanted out, or at least it was expected of me to want to get out, so I guess I made that getting-out my own wanting or expectation. Mum was from south London and she'd got out in her own way, at sixteen: went to Cardiff and sniffed out the burgeoning punk thing. This was in '75 I think. I remember her saying when she got to the Virgin Records store she was about to start managing, a few years later, right next to the front door was a fat papier mâché fly agaric mushroom with headphones dangling out of it's frills and beanbags at the base for the stoned hippy kids to zone out on, still listening to Cream. Her first day on the job she tore the whole thing down with a hammer. I was raised in the mythology of her life. It was never about feeling divisible from the people I grew up with. Most of them wanted out, too.

Delaney goes on to say:

> 'Since there was no permanent, externally
> agreed-on social organisational structure,

it's accurate to say that everything that happens in the commune was because of "your" or "my" whim. But "you" and "I" lived so close that the effect of "your" whim on "me" or "my" whim on "you" was immediately apparent. And there was no way to avoid responsibility for it. I worked, I ate, I bathed, I shit, I fucked, I went to sleep, and I woke up in the same room with you. There were no rooms you were not in. In that situation, it is impossible for me to allow you to do more work than you're comfortable doing, as you look around and see what is to be done; as you see what I'm doing; or what she or he is doing; or as you decide what, by whim, you feel like doing. That outraged hostility you experience when you have been socially mistreated, with which you can freeze a whole room of strangers, much less friends, just by walking into it in the right mood, I cannot tolerate when I am sleeping in the same bed you're balling in, when I'm balling in the same bed she's sleeping in, when she sits down on a toilet seat he's just left warm, when he's leaning against your leg while he eats, when I can feel your back muscles moving against mine while you eat. I do not believe in telepathy'.[12]

This is my favourite passage in the book. I love the way Chip makes the semicolons, the quotation marks and the interchangeable pronouns completely intradependent on one another. You take one phrase out and the whole thing turns to mush.

I don't romanticise this kind of life. How could I? It is absolutely unattainable. Or at least, even if it were attainable, haven't I been marinated too long in the 21st century; in total individuation? Could I stand the complete absence of even the faintest *idea* of personal space, or of solitude? I want to believe that I could shed it, I've shed lots of things. But I think it's important to draw a line here, as Delaney does, between The Commune — which *The Breakfast* ostensibly is — and the The Co-operative — which it definitionally isn't. The Co-operative is more resilient to the manifold violence of the world, and to austerity, in that it can successfully integrate itself into capital and is thereby more attainable. I might even be able to live in a cooperative if I wanted; if I could bear to sign up to yet another waiting list — not for a pussy this time but a roof over my head. None of this changes the fact that the conditions for a Commune with a capital C just don't currently exist in the urban spaces of this country.

I believe in cities as a social formation. I believe in the decrepit metropolitan as a stinking, gorgeous and absolutely fucked medley of absolutely cacophonous everything; I believe in staying close to the seat of power and not sequestering yourself from it; I believe in not believing that you can be divisible from it — from power; I believe in not believing that the city is dead and unliveable; or at least I believe that I don't want to let Them win — to cede ground; I believe in durable networks of interrelation because my friends are what keep me alive. What keeps me estrogenized. *There were no rooms you were not in.* I grew up in the country and the mythology of the city, of my mum's London, was all I had. I don't want to believe that following this mythology made me a class traitor, but I do wonder whether leaving your hometown does something irreparable to your class-consciousness. D talks about being the first person to write a book about your hometown that the people you grew up with won't hate you for. Am I worthy to speak on behalf of my past? No matter how sane or crazy? Hilton Als says 'What is there but other people?[13]' and he's right. *I can feel your back muscles moving against mine while you eat.*

~DROLATIC DREAMS &
REVOLUTIONARY AMBIVALENCE

i

Mikhail Bakhtin only had one leg. This crucial piece of information about his life is often overlooked.

ii

A reprimanded scholar, a bookseller, an exile and an amputee, Bakhtin understood the body firstly as a point of departure; the theatre of the first revolution. This was the revolution before all revolutions — the centrifuge of the carnival.

The renaissance carnival inverted the world. It was not an official celebration of a nation or deity, but a folk festivity which crowned a fool as king. Its hallmarks were feasting and excess, drink and debauchery, hyperbole in every sense.

Under the inverting rite of these festivities, the bodies of the folk became borderless, and blended into the bodies of the people and animals around them. Because they were no longer individuated subjects, the whole world could be filtered through their mouths and anuses. By letting things in, by expelling other things, the limits of the body were transgressed and exceeded.

iii

These were openings but also conjoinings. Unlikely mésalliances. High and low, rich and poor, virtuous and debased — these dualisms were not dissolved, but smashed into one another. Unseated from hierarchy, they reunited in ambivalent, drunken, carnal relativity. What does it mean to crown a fool as king?

iv

Bakhtin studied Rabelais and saw the carnival within Gargantua. He called it Grotesque. Not as a judgement but as an incitement to revelry.

During this time of carnival, masks were prevalent. The Grotesque loves a loose mouth and protruding nose. Among processions and at feasting tables mask-wearing was commonplace; identities were obscured but also reinforced. The expressions of the masks were immutable. They rang out cool and clear over the rippling tapestry of the face's subjectivity.

The old works of Rabelais were lost, and had to be unearthed.

v

Workers, cleaning the ditches near the sluices of the Vienne, inadvertently uncovered the entrance to a tomb. The tomb was inconceivably long and made of bronze. Deep inside, nine flagons were found arranged in the formation of a game of skittles. Under the central flagon, written on elm-bark, the labourers found a book. It was huge, greasy and grey. Pretty, too.

> *ai? . . . great conqueror of the Cimbri*
> *V . . . ing through the air, in terror of the dew,*
> *' . . . his arrival every tub was filled*
> *) . . . fresh butter, falling in a shower*
> *== . . . ith which, when the great ocean was*
> *bespattered*

This riddle, found on the first page of the book, was intentional nonsense, and had been nibbled at by vermin, to leave gaps in its meaning. But it didn't mean that a sense of something couldn't be imparted.

vi

Anathema to the Grotesque body was the body of the 'new canon' — the bodily canon of art, belles lettres and polite conversation. This body was closed, individuated and tightly bordered. It spoke in its name alone.

Because it was singular, all the events that took place inside this body could acquire only one meaning. Death meant only death. *Blows merely hurt, without assisting the act of birth.*

vii

Both Rabelais and Bakhtin lived and wrote during periods in which the limits of the world were being tested and remade. The Renaissance and the Russian Revolution each sought to induce absolute inversions of societal organisation, culture and human potential, but also invited precarity and flux — as well as the danger of a violent contraction.

The literary scholar Michael Holquist believed that in response to the unprecedented potentialities of these contexts, Rabelais and Bakhtin each 'created a special kind of open text that they explored as a means of inscribing themselves into their times'.[14]

viii

In 1940 Mikhail Bakhtin wrote:

"The grotesque body [...] is a body in the act of becoming. It is never finished, never completed; it is continually built, created, and builds and creates another body.

"The body that figures in all the expressions of the unofficial speech of the people is the body that fecundates and is fecundated, that gives birth and is born, devours and is devouring, drinks, defecates, is sick and dying.

"This is why the essential role belongs to those parts of the grotesque body in which it outgrows its own self, transgressing its own body, in which it conceives a new, second body: the bowels and phallus.

"All these convexities and orifices have a common characteristic; it is within them that the confines between bodies and between the body and the world are overcome: there is an interchange and an interorientation.

"The grotesque conception of the body is inter-woven not only with the cosmic but also with the social, utopian, and historic theme, and above all with the theme of the change of epochs and the renewal of culture.

"It is a point of transition in a life eternally renewed.

"The mighty material bodily element of these images uncrowns and renews the entire world of mediaeval ideology and order, with its belief, its saints, its relics, monasteries, pseudo-asceticism, fear of death, eschatologism, and prophecies.

"The grotesque seeks to grasp in its imagery the very act of becoming and growth, the eternal incomplete unfinished nature of being.

"In the Middle Ages [...] the earth, consisting of mountains and precipices, was constructed like a grotesque body. The impenetrable surface of the earth was constantly broken up by a tendency to rise or descend into the depths, into the underworld. In these depths and orifices another world was believed to exist.

"The human body becomes a building material. The limits between the body and the world are weakened.[15]

ix

'Rabelais plays with words', wrote the poet and novelist Anatole France, 'as children do with pebbles; he piles them up into heaps'.[16]

x

This body which exceeds itself to become the whole world is incapable of speaking in its name alone.

To speak Gargantua is also to say

(gar) (gan) (tu) (a)
mouth, abyss, thirst, folk

This plural voice, or chorus, announces a collective hunger.

~PUT YOUR HEAD UNDER THE
WATERLINE

In the morning you fuck me with my own dick

and out the window, clouds fume

with the dreamy nacre of old shallots

Your thighs

I'll say it again it's December

Right at the year's cusp

So the days are weighted, ambrosial

and they roll in languidly, like bitumen

shot through with white pith

under a luxurious

velvet curtain

~AND HEAR THE CONVERSATIONS OF YOUR NEIGHBOURS DOWNSTAIRS

In the curtain
I read pathos
and the ceilings of three hundred days jut out like spurs
I have hardening in me
and I guess we'll fiddle until everything is empty
as if you can ever scrub life from a place
Dark weals of routine
inviolable, sparkling
soft welts of heavy furnishings
the sequins, the sewing needles
spun through the very first layer of carpet
I twist them on my hands and knees
doubled over
til each of their tips point north

~THEY ARE MUFFLED THROUGH
THE WALL

Outside, the frost diffuse
like Stendhal
a tom-tits claw
all gloss
skinny bow thrown down a salt mine, deep
to ossify, he says, like pining:
slimly contoured and hoary
right beneath the sod
lousy with dry rustlings, just
over the way

The fat black douche, bereft
that was left on the sill
got spun through like hellweed —
little spiders live in it
A letter for nobody in particular arrives
There are chains, a t-shirt, nailed to the wall
Small drunk nooks of dusk jag out

~SOMETIMES A BATH CAN BE RUN SO HOT THAT IT BECOMES EXTRASENSORY

Caught the blurred photo of the caramel foal

right as she reached the gate,

ten years back:

fourteen chestnut

eyes and warm flanks all rippled with want

Leaned over the steel bar steaming, a lark!

apocryphal and

vital,

shit-at-heel

~PASS, ALL PASS

Girl,
she purred
{whinnying}
You brick —
Come
be your own stitch
Be the garbling

She is walking on a very narrow ridge, up high. The landscape resembles but is not a coastal hiking trail in the southwest of England. On her left side the ground gives way to a deep valley blistered with rich, dark verdancy. A river threads its way along the central crease, snaking its way between cracks in the foliage like a slim fillet of silver. The sun is neither bright nor dim. It is not entirely overcast nor necessarily clear. Light broaches the headland of her skull with the flat, eerie quality which most dreams retain, as if what is taking place remains outside of time, when really we are being made witness to something not quite distinguishable in either past or future tense, but rather the inimitable and permanent present of unconscious syntax.

Two large black labradors trot on either side of her. Because they are flanking her, they represent both Compassion (left) and Brute Force (right). She knows this because their formation denotes her as part of the pack.

When looking left, down into the valley, she is up high but still within a parameter of space which she recognises and can chart. But when looking right the land completely falls away: she is up, up, up impossibly high, thousands of feet high, viewing the landscape as if from a plane, or the summit a mountain. She is up so high that the land itself abstracts into an unfolding map; off-white, bisected by gridded black lines, red and green vertices, and occasional gestural flourishes which indicate rivers, their tributaries. Clouds rush over it.

Buried deep underneath the impossible plateau of the the map lies the last servers of what we now know as the internet, underground. She knows this intuitively. They are hardened, militarised, dormant and very powerful. They blink soberly and bathe the deep caverns in a sultry red glow. Already she knows that she will never see them, and she won't.

The ridge she is walking along slowly collapses towards the sea which lies at the base of the valley. The water does not stretch out onto the horizon, but lapses into nothing a little beyond the headland. At her furthest left the cliffs sag into the shape of a man lying down; his head, nose and shoulders jut above the tideline, slipping into the water like a shallow bath.

A minute or so in front of her down the path, a pale woman with deep red hair called Mary who she really barely knows wears a black jacket. Despite their distance they are walking together. She cannot see her face but she knows who she is. Mary does not beckon her, but continues down the path slowly, with intention; knowing that eventually she and the two dogs will catch up.

She reaches the bottom of the valley. Mary first, then her, and the two dogs soon after. As she steps out onto the beach she realises that it is a single rough shelf of glass, like it had once been made of sand before being hit by a wave of apocryphal heat.

Great black boulders pockmark the bay. Cold, bright water slaps against their hulls and through the roughly textured tracts and warrens of the glass. She splashes through the shallows following the woman while the dogs run wide circles around them both, disappearing between the clatter before momentarily re-emerging, salty-wet and steaming.

At some point she loses sight of the woman between the house-sized boulders and the wash of the deepening tide. One dog, she's not sure whether it is left or right, slips into a glass tunnel bored straight through the rock wall ahead. The other dog lingers behind her back; its eyes are yellow and beckon her forwards. There is no other way around. She crouches into the icy water and begins crawling through the tunnel, only a few feet across, on her hands and knees. Within seconds she can't feel her fingers.

Inside, the walls are low; wet, shimmering and crystalline. She hears the second dog entering the tunnel behind her, his paws shuffle through the clear water. She glances ahead to the other end of the tunnel and sees

not   really any   thing   at   all.

Then she is picking her way across a very large meadow and the dogs are nowhere to be seen. The woman, Mary, she is also gone. She is still in the southwest of England or at least inside an overlapping sheaf of memories which occurred there, but not actually within the spatial remit of their recurrence.

The sky is almost black with storm she is going somewhere. Intent is in the furrow of the dream like sour light, like electricity, but her eventual destination is not revealed to her. The thickening clouds are very heavy and streaked across the sky in tempered charcoal bands. Slightly lavender, smudged; the colour of muscle-shell. Everywhere she looks her vision is framed in two black circles — like how they used to represent someone looking through binoculars in cartoons or old movies.

Behind her, a single pylon juts out of the field colossally. The wind is rising and the meadow is filled with long barley which prostrates itself before the black pressure pouring out of the sky. It's stems part to make way for the lashes of the wind, like geese unzipping the water of a pond behind them.

Then suddenly lightning strikes the pylon and its bigger than anything; bigger and longer and more ripping than any lightning she's ever seen. The light spits about the tip of the mast for a sliver and then detonates. Within seconds the whole thing catches fire and somehow she films all of it — or begins filming just before the blaze takes hold. It is absolute volume, light, pressure, force.

She doesn't remember running away from the fire, down the country lane as the rain begins, but within the slippage of the dream she did. At her back a deep orange glow throbs into the firmament like a bruise. The rain grows unflinching, torrential. She can hear its low thrum nagging at her heels, half a mile behind.

Finally she finds herself in a living room with several people who feel close to her but who she doesn't look at close enough to recognise. She tries to show the video of the lightning strike by uploading it to Youtube and then playing it on the TV. But the circle spins round and round and its gone from her phone somehow, as if it didn't exist but it did.

~SIDEWINDER

Honestly don't

even try me you won't ever know the absolute

blister / of

the contusion of what's coming My

bed / stinks

it's still warm from when I left it

Promised myself I would never write from the pose, the

facile thorn of spite

and I'll keep that

Suck / spit

it's the way the light hits; injecting

slow down the globby strand, thick Like silver it

slips from the black furrows   .

filigreed between my

teeth / Words

are often food to me and that's bad Saw a strap hung on

the wall in a gallery the hung prick the leg, the hoof of a

fawn and got a

little / wet

Went back home tonight for no reason

felt little only

a flat assuredness that whatever wounding I might try

to bum off this place could not

actually / split

me because Really

nothing can undo the

white / bones

of my forearms the

woman's shaft sheafed beneath between my thighs the

breasts I'll cup to transmute some warmth cordoned

like doves

under the armpit

Snuck into the garden and cowed low under the lamp

all frozen, the grass solid, cold

so / frozen

that frost was on I mean *in* the window, strung like a

slender dremeling Their

glib / warmth;

all comfortably upwardly middle class and it's all so

nice you know the repointed brickwork

Walked around the woods at the back, found

the spot where I'd broken

down on all fours in the mud that April and threw

myself up so late The

snot it all

pooled / heaving

in claggy furrows I'd clawed through The air

on the turn from spring to summer

rancid / raggedy

in big whooping gasps, deep

syphoning the night Before I left I drank

two / tins

in the park and just absolutely unpeeled so Take

the tarnished coins off my eyes, lids

flicker as they're prised apart Together

see the two welts left by a blind gauze, *no*, gaze

unflinching

face / it

all fucking down as they drilled for

what they thought was the last time over the jaunty

fence into the blacked out windows where something

      once lived

And it's so strange you know what you can't

find when you look for it

A crow caws like the old woman I hope to become and

silently I throw

sticks / shards

of ice on the black frozen lens

of the lake

under the slip moon total like cocaine The big ZAP and

the drawn-out tinkering as little

slivers of itself

skitter across

the disc

Good / words

are failing me Lose

four hundred yards to the sentences unlatching from my

gait / suddenly

I'm at my door, key fiddling The

furious pace at which I've crawled back to my hovel five

minutes away So

close the four

bed ex-council the sublet thank fuck it's

real / Here

under the sheets and the dim glow of the screen letters

leave me; retracted

like my spit as I renounce it Spooled off the

plump / root

hacked back up just before it touches two tonsils So

kindly you say

       she

softly / your

hand on my shoulder, correcting

the small man who will soon bawl openly like a child

before

he starts swinging Had to drag

him to the ground my arm around his neck he

spat you filthy drag queen which I smirked at even

while I thought he might tear

through my grip and

bludgeon / me

with the fire extinguisher

The tears on your face I couldn't stand it He

went for the Christmas tree and Adam said That's It

threw him back

out into the snow, on his hands and knees

hogtied / steaming

lost / Where

he belonged Duds offered

to get their brother's mates round but

we barricaded the door with

five bikes Smoked two cigs screamed Get away from the

windows and almost

passed / out

Can't believe we called the police, the guilt

how to deal with such terror

abolitionistically Heard him bawl I was attacked by two

giant lesbians while he was getting nicked because they

left us on speaker

and we laughed grimly

All in five

minutes / Cookies

out the oven The complete camp farce of actually

having a genuinely wholesome

time before a foot goes through a reinforced glass

door / Cher

says *I'm freezing to death* Nicholas

Cage says *there will be nothing left* I

guess it's easier to metabolise things as a group but

"The Ravishment"

          his

mouth on her neck I can't stop

thinking about it Imagine the blood and posit, like a

plum / pit:

do I want to be eaten by an apex predator to know that
I could just die unlucky?
A rending only Total
fatal violence devoid of intention or bigotry
mute, languageless
there was no
need for her to die this way she was
simply / Unlucky
in the cast sense, like a die
Cold and Logically Totalising, Primal,
Wretched, Fair, Unflinching and not without
Purpose / viciousness
has it's

uses you know it's all in
the / meat
So take me out back like ol' yeller I honestly think I
might be unkillable the way glamour forms a carapace
about me
buffed so hard it gleams like a mirror Fanny Howe says
it / (glamour)
removes any possible chance of reciprocity
which is a huge relief[17]
so Catch your breath as you snatch a look trepidatiously
in the windows of parked cars
for the returned shadow of a bitch unmaking
lick split lips festooned with stain It'll
only ever reflect back the grimace of those who

can't / own

me I'll never stop I won't ever stop I'll abruptly snap

again please

multiply my confoundedness

        Lord! un —

cowl me / from the enrobing of another's need that I am

perfectly articulated in

To earnestly give more than you possibly can is an

intractable violence

so / don't

let me apologise while I become literal

the mundanity of inalterable drift

Wan smirk of the ice on the low roof makes me bite my

cheek two

planes wink out under the

weak / sun

as their course changes A fox heckles me as I turn my

back eventually and I smile

because I know I him left a steel

dish of water outside the den that

summer everything

started / dying

I'll

kill

the

cop

in

side

my

self and

go one further We are Each

Coming / For

God in our own maniacal pursuit of the anarchic

carnivalesque But

I am an insuppressible maniac who is glad for the

source of

my / chaff

It soothes me The

chaff of my life Like really I could not tell you quite

how I am alive *Hello yes baby*

hold onto my wrist

just watch me

un-cum myself with a rag stitched in an imbroglio of

succubic piss Each

child scattered a blue plastic bag

from the offy

bursting with peonies Felt the hot wind on my legs,

prickly, naked *What*

a lovely girl I hold my mum's hand

outside the post office *Yes*

the young lady at the back Hot face in my hands in

the school

auditorium Small tears

bark out quick Take it

all back

I will

go

grasping through the years

gritty orifices, so

giving / pliable

I promise you By

the years of being retraced, generously by

being fucked, so generously So

many

fucked

years

the / fingering

Like picking at the now-nothing fizz of an old

scab-gone-scar so white but

never / blending

because Truly I am sick I am puking I am completely

unbecoming Watch me unravel; unravel each please

putridly tear your seams with me We are only as long as

our own

      shared delirium

      like / gossamer

      Each poem

is its own kind of failure

2~

DISQUIET DRIVE

I have tried to write this essay so many times. Each new draft burrows through the old one and disperses, or kind of chews it up. Always the feeling is one of clawing-through. Once a new draft begins I have to erase the old one, for fear that its language will inflect the writing of the day to come. At times I become impossibly frustrated, and turn instead to reading, taking the top of the sour duvet in my teeth and biting down.

Lately I've been thinking a lot about disquiet. Disquiet as a sensation in the body and the language that gives it silhouette. That makes it physical. Disquiet as a poetics and a revolutionary tool: and as an offensive position. Really I want to praise disquiet. I want to write a paean to the tremor of not-sitting-right, to be driven back into unease and the pain of it. It is familiar to me. That sounds sadomasochistic and of course on some level it is, but such wounding is necessary. Eventually you have to grapple with your own continuity. If only because there is information there — a lake of it.

I agonise over these drafts because I have not been honest with myself; honest with the material. I actually do not know if I can sustain or contain myself within the lyric essay as a form. It does not feed me. Bits of my language flake off to appease it, I give over, I give up. I surrender something to the syntax, the pose, of a class position that was not my birthright, and which I resisted my attempted inculcation in — though of course on occasion the mask would slip, and, immolating myself, I would attempt to make up for it. Writing as a vector of shame. Coherence as an appeasement. To whom? To language itself? Whose language?

I know now that I have no one I need to prove myself to. That my words gutter out when attempting to mimic a style built on a set of material, temporal and sexual conditions to which I will never have access. The more of my life passes, the poorer I become, the more time slips away from me, the less logical the world seems, the less sense I make to myself, and I am glad for it because this emptying of coherence forced me to uncoil the impossibly compressed spider that I was. Ambiguity as a means of resistance. Fuck off as an inoculation against assimilation.

I came very close to that slow death, acquiescing to a language not made for me, because there are scant few ways to avoid it: to skirt professionalism or a softening of the edges, to not have a job; to abdicate from or get outside of a very pernicious momentum in speech and learning. Truthfully I felt safe there, close to that morbidity — cosseted in the reassuring but actually impossibly precarious nest of an aspirational language and a seemingly congruent body that I could not convincingly perform and had no alignment with. And so the rampant notes I hammered across the margins of earlier drafts of this essay, the prickling whispers which nicked me in the margins of the night, began to make sense in a way my agonised, inoffensive paragraphs and my meek, self-abasing life never could. Simply I must dispense with the expectation to make meaning. I must not wait for permission. And I need to put myself at risk.

This essay orbits around three rich white women who each practised a form of self-immolation: Simone Weil, Chris Kraus, Kathy Acker. Each of these women attempted to withdraw from the body as a site of individuated meaning to quell a kind of disquiet they felt in their physicality. Femininity has something to do with it, they each say, about themselves and about one another. Illness, too. Particularly the kind of illness that does not have clearly delineated symptoms or a definitive resolution in time. Anorexia as a pathology and as a formal diagnosis is thrown around, in good faith and sometimes ahistorically. Language stands in for bodies, bodies are drilled for language, words stand in for food; contradictions emerge. These three bodies flicker and overlap, they seek resonances with one another, Kraus writes about them both and in turn writes about herself, there is so much time, time, time;

time to write, to reflect on, to worry over or to buy —
even to collapse a century with.

Let's face things exactly as they are. Weil was born a
month before term in 1909, in Paris, on the Boulevard
de Strasbourg. It was a beautiful building with intricate
tiling on its facade and a mascaron of a lion. Her
brother Andre received her coming cooly, later the
temperature would plummet. Acker, born Karen
Lehman but who at some point became Kathy, was
raised in Sutton Place on the Upper East Side. Her
family received a small fortune from her paternal
grandfather whose business had been making gloves.[18]
She attended Lenox School: a private all-girls institution
on the Upper East side until she was ostensibly
disowned in her teens, before receiving a substantial
inheritance in 1981. Kraus says "She hated, she envied,
she loved"[19] the bourgeoisie: the project of Acker's life
was to shatter their syntax.

For her part, Kraus was born to the Bronx in 1955 and
grew up in Connecticut until her parents emigrated to
New Zealand at the age of 15. Her father worked as a
publisher at both Macmillan and Cambridge University
Press. She is a landlord of several properties across low
income neighbourhoods in Albuquerque, New Mexico
— a practice she once described as 'a way of engaging
with a population completely outside the culture

industry. Kind of like in gay culture, where hookups are a way of escaping your class'.[20]

Why I, a white working class transexual woman am drawn toward these three rich white cis women is perhaps not a particularly interesting question with a very short answer. But still I need to answer it. I, too, have practised this same form of self-immolation. Like Weil and Kraus, I attempted to abdicate from my body as a site of meaning and used hunger as a means to achieve it. Like Acker, I spent years failing to hear the language of my body before finally finding something I could trust. Like each of these women I found it almost impossible to reconcile 'femininity' with my person, and for the longest time revoked it.

In *The Melancholia of Class: A Manifesto for the Working Class,* Cynthia Cruz writes:

> 'The original dandy is the symbol of the death drive: without any income, without a home, and yet dressed to kill. Like the anorexic, who is similarly without agency, who has similarly been pushed up against the wall, to the point of speechlessness, with nothing left to lose, the dandy has made of himself a symbol. He is a gesture; he has sublimated his overwhelming affects of rage and sorrow into this one act'.[21]

Cruz draws on Camus' *The Rebel* in this passage to reframe the dandy as a self-immolator. Like the anorexic, the dandy shunts the performance of a certain kind of normalcy past the point of farce. He performs neatness and presentability so perfectly that it becomes an absurd caricature of the very conformity originally associated with the style, and it's through self-denial and thinness that the anorexic does the same: accelerating herself beyond the relative expectations of the beauty standard into a realm of sickness and beleaguered self-perception. Both the dandy and the anorexic achieve a *too-muchness* by 'push[ing] through the values of the ruling class and end[ing] up somewhere else entirely'.[22] Yet whatever life exists in that third space, the ultimate destination of this *somewhere else* is death. Death by drugs or violence, death by starvation or its complications, death by a certain kind of generational nihilism — death by being dead. They are each driven towards it inexorably, diving deep into self-abnegation as a response to the untenability of their material conditions. Is the body itself not a material condition, the first one? And if the dandy and the anorexic are driven towards death, what does it mean to be driven toward disquiet? What is the disquiet drive?

The working class trans woman is a symbol of the disquiet drive. Her life is precarious, she is often without any income or stable home, she exists beyond the neoliberal paradigm of sublimation into work because, simply, she cannot be contained. She is unproductive both because she cannot or will not sell her labour via the normative channels, and because she occupies the untenable position of being a woman divisible from her reproductive capacity, which the state demands total sovereignty over. And yet she is dressed to kill. Like the anorexic, which indeed she may also be, she is without agency. She is up against the wall of a world which conceives of her existence as an aberration, and under that pressure of unmaking she may become speechless, to be without language, or to be unable to hear the language of her body, and so in response she makes of herself a symbol: an irrevocable carapace of glamour, an incontrovertible armour of womanhood that the manifold violence of the world cannot crack. All her rage and sorrow are sublimated into this affect. It makes her immutable, sacred. By which I mean that her body cannot be broken.

I suppose I am trying to burrow into her body. By which I mean Simone's body, the anorexic body; my body — which may in turn be any trans woman's body. To pick at the edges of these bodies as individuated subjectivities and go beyond them. And also to understand what happens when they collapse in on themselves.

Sometimes I am rocked by the feeling that we — transexual women, transfeminine people — each share the same body. I used to feel it more, now I feel it less. I feel this feeling fully in the knowledge that it is dangerous, unboundaried, leaky, assumptive, juvenile, amoral, unethical and absolutely perverse. When I say that we each share the same body I mean literally. Not because we may or may not be undergoing the same psychological, spiritual and physical revolutions; and not because — as we are most certainly — subject to the varying appellations of scrutiny, fetishisation and violence modulated by our intersectional differences; our ethnicity, access needs and class; the same composite anxieties, the misogyny and transmisogyny, the necropolitics. I mean literally that the borders of my body are not where it ends.

On the few occasions I've allowed myself to try and convey this feeling I've been met, at best, by polite deferral and at worst outright revulsion. This might be because I normally express it when I'm high. I'll cup a friend's ear on the dance floor and what follows is some version of "can we talk about this later?" — and without fail I am grateful for the quiet mercy of that answer. Because of course I am being insufferable, leaky, and — as my friends know me well enough to apprehend — this leakiness is but one irascible node in a greater matrix of overwrought desires, for kinship and belonging, that I have misdirected time and time again in my life. But still the feeling persists. It persists among women I know, women I don't, women with whom I feel no connection at all, women I don't even like, abstracted women that I don't know exist, women across the world that I'll never meet; the women gone before and the women to come. Some people respond and say that I am simply describing solidarity, but solidarity is the recognition that other people's needs are indivisible from your own, not that you and the other person are indivisibly the same. The feeling is perhaps not dissimilar from the type of 'empathy', this is Kraus' word for the sensation — though I'm not sure it is accurate — that she, as an anorexic, felt towards Simone Weil's body, similarly afflicted, through the long tracts of the years.

'How close can I get to someone? Will we become each other?'[23] Acker once asked Alan Sondheim. Kraus says, 'emotion is a current that dissolves the boundaries of a person's subjectivity. It is a country. Shouldn't it be possible to *leave* the body? Is it wrong to even try?'.[24]

If disquiet is the feeling that something is not quite right, that there is unease, a queasiness or a certain kind of lag, an irreconcilable discomfort; the need to exceed one's own skin or even to shrug it off entirely, then the disquiet drive is the urge to move through that condition of abjection and unease, anxiety, tension or entrapment, and drill down into it. To claw-through. As a formal methodology this burrowing — into Simone's body, Kraus' body, my body; three anorexic bodies, indeed perhaps all trans bodies — is perverse, undoubtedly, and it threatens to re-perform the very same issues I take with Acker and in turn Kraus's methodology: their syntax, the flattening of their class positionality, and the way they write about other women. The audacity and the leakiness. But I am also guilty of these same transgressions: of whittling empathy — what the blurb to Kraus' *Aliens & Anorexia* describes as 'the ultimate perceptive tool' — into a weapon, a kind of dagger of glass, to use upon others and also on yourself.

From *Aliens & Anorexia*:

> 'I identified with the dead philosopher completely. Like her, I had a chronic illness which made it difficult to eat. Both of us had long necks and shoulders that hunched forward when we walked, a clumsy eagerness that tried against all odds to break outside the limits of our awkward bodies. We both smoked hand-rolled cigarettes and had absolutely zero sense of our "femininity" or gender'.[25]

In the first few movements of this book, Kraus begins the project of making herself and Weil inextricable. Simone's health, her gestures, her anatomy and habits, repeated through Kraus, reinvoke her person: both pathologically (a chronic illness which makes it difficult to eat), anatomically (long necks, hunched shoulders), gesturally (a clumsy eagerness), and habitually (smoking hand-rolled cigarettes). Weil is perfectly articulated in the language of Kraus' body and through this concurrence becomes a tool that allows Kraus to better see herself. To perceive her own body clearer. I read this extract

and watch them walking

aside a river, astride

a small European city, in step,

the street cobbled; there is frost.

The river sluggish like

cooling slag.

All grey-black

and sepia.

Kraus in her blazer, open at the waist,

Simone in something woollen, voluminous

big buttons.

They walk in step sort of quickly and

their hair is whipped backwards by a March

wind and they both try desperately

to smoke despite

it.

Weil has been known first and foremost, Elizabeth Hardwick says, through 'paraphrasing' — by the abbreviation of her life and thought into 'dramatically reduced and vivid moments', each one like a panel of stained glass. These attenuations to her biography have become so pervasive that Simone eventually 'takes on the clarity of the very reduction itself',[26] and the results are self-evident. Often Weil seems accessible only through tracing the margins of someone else's judgement: 'The Martian'[27], that 'ludicrous female mystic'; 'a bad Jew', 'a manipulative anorexic'; 'the brilliant crazy girl, the awkward scarecrow in flat shoes, the self-loathing and self-starving androgyne'.[28]

All these names and monikers, half-truths and veiled-insults; they make a crust.

Weil failed at being a woman — that's what's alleged. Even Kraus asserts in this passage that both women have absolutely 'zero sense' of their gender, and it's true that by her late teens Simone had begun to eschew whatever performance of femininity had apparently been expected of her. From then on she was never seen to wear makeup again, routinely wore men's clothes, and '[gave] up any desire to think of herself as a woman or to be regarded as such by others'. At boarding school she even went so far as to 'speak of herself in the masculine gender and to sign her letters "your respectful son".[29] Her parents chidingly dubbed her Simon, for a time. So much of the vitriol directed at Simone both before and after her death was channelled through this aperture in sex; a lapse in which something was supposed to reside. Her brother Andre was a paragon of intellectual masculinity, there was a template. For Simone, what? A female mystic, in the 20th century? The premise was morally bankrupt. Even Kraus knew it was ludicrous. Francine du Plessix Gray, in her 2001 biography of Weil — a portrait Kraus describes as 'stunningly dismissive'[30] — writes:

> 'Simone's cross-dressing and her need to disfigure herself into a caricature of the beautiful girl she could have been were related to far darker, more tragic aspects of her personality: the despair caused by her general sense of unworthiness, her sense that she was plain and somehow incomplete and could not be loved as a woman, her deep unease about issues of gender'.[31]

Her own brother, in an 'extraordinarily patronising' introduction to Weil's essay *Poem of Force* — again it is Kraus who rushes to her defence — remarked that 'if only she had combed her hair, worn stockings and high heels, the world might have taken her more seriously'.[32]

The world, men; they have trouble reconciling fragile beauty with its abdication.

Simone was not innately brilliant, her brilliance was a freak consequence of her own perceived unworthiness, her unlovability: this seems to be the consensus. She was gifted, undoubtedly, but what was the nature of the gift? Where did it reside? Many people felt that she was not quite of the domain of the living. Shuttered in her parent's Paris apartment, she once argued even Trotsky into a stalemate. We know that Weil avoided physical touch her whole life, despite being enormously affectionate. As Kraus reminds us, Nancy Houston 'pities [Weil] because she didn't fuck'.[33] Like fetish scrutinised under a psychoanalytic lens, Simone's contributions to 20th century philosophy and mysticism can subsequently only be understood as a misdirected desire for completeness or for love; a desire displaced so strongly that it apparently demanded Weil submit to increasingly pernicious means of self-disfiguration.

Louis Bercher, a family friend of the Weil's, wrote the following after regaling Simone with the fate of a nun who ate very little, and nourished herself only on the eucharist:

> 'I had the sensation that I was both giving her pleasure and *doing her harm*. That was how it

> was with this creature who was at war with
> her own life. If you did one side of her good,
> you wounded the other side'.[34]

Weil's health, like her relationship with food, was unreliable for most of her life. Hardwick remarked that 'refusal seems to have been part of her character since infancy'.[35] While Simone was still a baby, her mother suffered an attack of appendicitis yet continued to nurse her, and Weil would later attribute this moment of transmission — from mother's breast to infant mouth; poisoned milk into a pure vessel — to her eventual decline. "That's why", she would say, "I am such a failure".[36] Kathy Acker, tailspinning in the wake of a rapidly metastasising cancer prognosis which, following her double-mastectomy, she did not pursue formal medical treatment for, swore her ill health began when she dropped her Evian bottle into Regent's Canal during a walk along the towpath. It was not cancer she claimed, again and again, but simply poisoned water.

> 'Often Weil spoke of her "disgustingness."
> When it was a question of doing certain things,
> she would say, "I can't, because of my
> disgustingness"'.[37]

Simone and Acker, like the sculptor Eva Hesse — their lives get scoured for meaning. Kraus felt that most secondary texts about Simone treated her philosophical writings as 'a kind of biographic key'[38] and Lucy Lippard notes that the same was true for Hesse, with 'her memory exploited even by those writers who purported to be seriously discussing her art'.[39] Lazy critics, we know, scour the particulars of a person's inner life to try and find something they can cling to — to render their work legible. Such an attitude is typified in this quote by Robert Smithson:

> 'Eva's work was very rational, but a struggle, with irrational forces threading through it. I think I was most interested in her perception of the world, her outlook. There was an understanding of the more troubled areas, a kind of natural comprehension — not sentimental — but sort of facing them. She had no external notion of a world outside of hers. I saw her as a very interior person making psychic models'.[40]

And so the female artist or writer whose interior life is scrutinised as the only adequate means of understanding her work is left in a situation where artists and critics alike become 'most interested in her perception of the world'. She is then framed as 'a very interior person' who has 'no external notion of a world outside of hers' and in which she 'struggles with irrational forces'.

Thankfully, she still has a feminine 'natural comprehension' to fall back on.

If Hesse confounded diminutions like these both through her very public relationship with psychoanalysis and what Lippard describes as "the sheer density of her confrontation with the materials of her life" — remarking in a 1970 interview with Cindy Nemser: "My life and art have not been separate. They have been together"[41] — then Simone did so by forcibly inscribing what she wrote into her physicality.

Of Weil, Kraus writes:

> '[She] was more a mystic than a theologian. That is, all the things she wrote were field notes for a project she enacted on herself. She was a performative philosopher. Her body was material'.[42]

In December 1934, at the age of 25, Weil took a leave of absence from teaching philosophy at a private all-girls school in Le Puy to work in an automobile factory for the next year. Mostly she operated the milling machine. Warm curls of steel unwound at her feet like dying flies. In 1936 she travelled to Spain to join the anarchist Durutti Column during the Spanish Civil War. By September she had been asked to leave. Come

While Kraus understood this rejection of sustenance as a 'rejection of the cynicism our culture hands us through our food',[53] it seems only natural to wonder whether she needed Simone's self-starvation to mean something more than it did. She was, after all, attempting to 'reclaim anorexia from the psychoanalytic girl-ghetto of low self-esteem', hoping to show that refusing to eat could be understood as more than 'a desire for mortification'[54] — that it was propelled by an intuition that didn't go *further than sense could follow*, but rather somewhere else entirely. I've often hoped this for myself, too.

In 1945, Weil published *The Iliad, or The Poem of Force*.

> 'He is alive; he has a soul; and yet — he is a thing. An extraordinary entity this — *a thing that has a soul*. And as for the soul, what an extraordinary house it finds itself in! Who can say what it costs it, moment by moment, to accommodate itself to this residence, how much writhing and bending, folding and pleating are required of it? It was not made to live inside a thing; if it does so, under pressure of necessity, there is not a single element of its nature to which violence is not done'.[55]

Force, for Weil, was the true subject of the *Iliad*. 'It is that X that turns anybody who is subjected to it into a thing'[56] — meaning that we can only read the presence of what's been lost in the traces left: dwindling cold baths or empty chariots rattling through the fields of battle. Defeated on the battlefield, supplicant and clasping at his knees, Hector implores Achilles to spare his life:

> 'Thus spoke the brilliant son of Priam
> In begging words. But he heard a harsh reply:
> He spoke.
> And the other's knees and heart failed him.
> Dropping his spear, he knelt down, holding out
> his arms.
> Achilles, drawing his sharp sword, struck
> through the neck and breastbone.
> The two-edged sword sunk home its full
> length. The other, face down, lay still and
> the black blood ran out, wetting the ground'.[57]

Hector remains Hector in this passage, before Achilles replies. He speaks, is brilliant, is named, is doing — as in the present participle of *begging* — but at the very instant that Achilles opens his mouth, even before his tongue begins to shape the sentence which condemns him to death, Hector becomes a corpse. From then on, Hector is referred to only as 'the other' and is described as such before Achilles' blade ever meets his neck. Now unable to utter I, Hector's 'extraordinary house' drops its spear and submits to the 'writhing and bending, folding and pleating' required of it — because it is a soul living in a house, not a home. Susan Howe:

> 'Iliadic   heroism   another
> situation   of   unstable
> identity'[58]

Weil believed she might experience the Spanish Civil as she had the Greek epics, says Kraus. Before she joined the Durutti Column in 1936, Weil petitioned the Partido Obrero de Unificación Marxista to let her go undercover in a one-woman rescue mission to bring back Joaquin Maurin, the Party's founder, from Franco territory. The POUM abjectly refused: she was too white to pass as Spanish, and had zero experience with firearms or espionage. There was no way she would make it out alive. Gorkin, the international secretariat of the party and Maurin's brother in law, told her 'you would have a ninety percent chance of sacrificing yourself for nothing' — to which Weil became incensed, demanding that 'she had every right to sacrifice herself if she wished'.[59]

She would later write:

> 'If the I is the only thing we truly own, we
> must destroy it. *Use the I to break down I*'.[60]

Simone was, in the words of Anne Carson, 'a person who wanted to get herself out of the way to arrive at God'.[61] By the 1930s Weil had come to believe that the 'I' occupied a perspectival centre that was untenable, because it obstructed a person's ability to connect with God. This obstruction, in turn, interrupted God's ability to connect with the world. Selfhood was offered by God as a gift, but by accepting this gift a person became irreparably distanced from him. This problem was inescapable — like how children say the word *Now* over and over again to try and capture proof of their own persistence in time. The only way to get closer to God, then, was to withdraw from the I and its body entirely: thereby offering back up to God what had originally been bestowed upon her.

> 'We possess nothing in this world other than the power to say "I." This is what we must yield up to God. God can love in us only this consent to withdraw in order to make way for him'.[62]

Simone called it 'undoing the creature in us', or more generally 'decreation' — a term she coined but never gave a singular explanation for. To abdicate from the body in order to make way for God and the world, like three jealous lovers, a couple and a third — Carson called it 'three people trying to sit in two chairs'.[63]

> 'If only I knew how to disappear there would be a perfect union of love between God and the earth I tread, the sea I hear . . .'[64]

It's easy to read this sentence as proof of Weil's self-immolatory intent. Her detractors, as we've seen, so often did. Marya Hornbacher, in her 1997 *Wasted: A Memoir of Anorexia and Bulimia*, writes:

> 'The awful paradox is that, to me, it seemed that my emotional survival, my basic personal integrity, was dependent upon my mastery, if not total erasure, of my physical self'.[65]

What's unendingly complicated about Weil is that even if she was trying to get outside herself, to break down her I or offer it back up to God, she was adamant that doing so was a compassionate expression of love — a perfect union of love. She abdicated from the body because she wanted, not necessarily to be loved, but to be a vessel *for* love. Richard Rees:

> "Like all the mystics, Simone Weil tells us that it is only by destroying the I that it becomes possible to

106

fully believe in, and therefore truly love, the existence of anything outside ourselves'.[66]

If someone believes so ardently that hollowing out their body is the only way to fill it up with God — with love — if they consider that hollowing to be a compassionate gesture towards themselves, then should we not at least listen to them on their own terms? On the surface, this is what Kraus was attempting to do: treat Simone's self-starvation as a serious philosophical project of love by putting her writing before her biography, any mythology, or the pathological designation of Weil as solely 'an anorexic philosopher', as the textbooks state.[67] Yet Kraus couldn't stop herself from reproducing this same binary — self-hating anorexic or honest-to-God mystic — even as she attempted to reclaim anorexia from the psychoanalytic girl-ghetto of low self-esteem.[68] She could not get outside of this debate because she was culpable in it, too.

Hilton Als:

'During the Marie years and for some time after, I looked at physical love like an anorexic looking at food: I did not understand how to consume it while I wanted nothing more than to consume it. Like everyone else, I required love's nutrients — its touch — but didn't that spoil love? To put one's body in it? To not claim it — to not grab it by the short of the hair, or by its wit — was, to this Simone Weil of the ghetto at least, the greater good: why could we not rise up out of the world of bodies? Rise up and be holy, holy, holy, in the oneness of love'.[69]

This love. I do not agree with Als' construction of the anorexic as not understanding food and yet *wanting nothing more than to eat,* as if anorexia is solely defined by a masochistic relationship between the promise of satiation and its fulfilment, and not a stasis in which desire detaches itself from the very idea of promise *or* fulfilment, (Kraus calls anorexia 'a violent breaking of the chain of desire')[70] but I will concede that Simone did not know how to offer love while wanting nothing more than to give it. I will say that she spent her whole life — fervently, unflinchingly — trying to work out how to love without *putting her body in it*; attempting to *rise up out of the world of bodies*, and thereby arrive at love. And is that not the tragedy of her life, even though her life was defiantly, grimly, so much more than a tragedy? Can we not admit the role of tragedy just as it was, as an aperture into love? Als is talking about romantic love in this paragraph, or at least the love of a twin, and so perhaps the comparison is trite — but Simone seems to have had no quantifiable interest in romantic love whatsoever. Instead, her love was enormous, absolutely diffuse: a beneficent love for every down-and-out and wretch, every dandy and self-immolator, a love that was its own knife of empathy, in which — lacerating every kind of boundary — what she *saw* became what she'd *been through*. It would be impossible for this love which so enraptured Simone to ever be channelled through one single person. That would have demanded Weil not only become love's recipient, but also to submit her own body as being the object of another's love. To fill her body up with love and not cynicism or the world or the suffering of others. Under such a loving gaze, who could help but become an I? To *put her own body in it*?

'Without love it is impossible to eat', says Kraus. 'When I can't eat it's because I feel totally alone'.[71]

Midway through *Aliens*, after discussing Sartre's *The Emotions: Outline of a Theory*, Kraus writes:

> '[...] why do Weil's interpreters look for hidden clues when she argues [...] for a state of decreation? She hates herself, she can't get fucked, she's ugly. If she finds it difficult to eat, it must be that she's refusing food, as anorexics do, as an oblique manipulation. "The girl" in Sartre and Janet's narrative breaks down in

order to gain sympathy and draw attention. Anything a female person says or does is open to "interpretation". If the female anorexic isn't consciously manipulative, then she's tragic: shedding pounds in a futile effort to erase her female body, which is the only part of her that's irreducible and defining'.[72]

Kraus is not just parroting Simone's detractors here, nor is she blindly reinvoking the dismissiveness of Sartre, Plessix-Gray, or Andre as a window into the denigration Simone must have experienced during her life and after it. Instead, she is offering us a new kind of doubling. Kraus intimately understands the way in which such vitriol *works:* if she finds it difficult to eat, it *must* be that she's refusing food, *as anorexics do,* as *an oblique manipulation.* Each point in the progression of this logic is sharply pinned in place. This is the finality of arguing against someone who's already made up their mind about who you are, or what your body means. Then there's the emphatic rattling off of 'She hates herself, she can't get fucked, she's ugly' — each phrase like a slap in the face — and the singular, standalone sentence, 'Anything a female person says or does is open to "interpretation"', with interpretation notably in quotation marks. Whether to draw attention to the shaky premise of objectivity bound up in that word, or literally as an invocation of a demeaning word from a friend, lover, parent or partner, is left for us to decide. Just as Simone is a tool which allows Kraus to see her own body clearer, she also speaks through Weil to shield herself from harm.

What remains so intriguing about this paragraph is its final line: 'her female body, which is the only part of her that's irreducible and defining' — a far cry from the twinned anorexics who where once described as having 'zero sense of their "femininity" or gender'. Kraus lurches repeatedly between these two positions in *Aliens:* between understanding her body as an androgynous vessel of pure spirit and as an indissoluble bearer of the burden of femininity, its physicality. Does Kraus think of herself as a woman? She rejects in all manner of ways the patriarchal prescriptions of femininity that are imposed upon her, as she should, as well as any traditional conflation of eating disorders with 'feminine' laments of narcissism or vanity. She rejects all this much as she rejects food 'and everything else at the most cellular level'.[73]

Yet Kraus also rebukes the 'polemically feminist' framing of anorexia among teenage girls as a deferral of their reckoning with a prescribed social gender. It is not sex-gender systems themselves that get divested of meaning here, but rather their primacy; with Kraus withering any argument in which 'the formation of a gender-based identity is still the primary animating goal in the becoming of a person, if that person is a girl'.[74] The problem is not about being a girl intrinsically, but in being *nothing but* a girl.

> 'So long as anorexia is read exclusively in relation to the subject's feelings towards her own body, it can never be conceived as an active, ontological state [...] It's inconceivable that the female subject might ever simply try to *step outside* her body, because the only thing that's irreducible, still, in female life is gender'.[75]

Something else is required to explain anorexia it seems. Something else. And I agree with her. Everywhere people try to explain Kraus' body to her; try to force her to eat. Pathologies and misogyny proliferate. The doctor says this, the spiritualist says that. A friend or a lover or a husband says something else, and she says No. Or at least, Fuck Off. But still there is a sense that at the core of Kraus' refusal of any singular prescription of femininity is its conflation with beauty: to be too glamorous, too gorgeous, is to open oneself up to vapidity and narcissism — or at least the perception by others of you, largely men, as vain or narcissistic — an untenable position, irrespective of it's creeping misogyny, for an author committed to being seen to *write about other people.*

But perhaps I am the one being misogynistic, by working to reignite the premise that some significant part of anorexia may really be about presentation, or about being perceived. I'm happy to ignite this claim because it is a criticism often levied at transexual women too. The glamorous woman, the anorexic, the trans woman: we are each self-obsessed, image-obsessed, we care about no one else but ourselves; so acute is the internal strife that we feel that we have no heed of any suffering beyond the borders of our own bodies. Is that not what people say about us? That we do not on some level internalise and naggingly agonise over about ourselves, despite all evidence to the contrary? And if the transexual is *also* anorexic? If she is gorgeous? God help her.

Kraus notes that many of Weil's biographers find it predictably 'impossible to conceive of a female life that may extend outside itself. Impossible to accept the self-destruction of a woman as strategic'[76] — as if the two come as a pair, like giving pleasure and doing harm. And are they not? At least for the anorexic, does she — was I — not trying to extend outside our bodies — my body — by collapsing inwardly, by refusing food? Is Kraus not trying to extend outside of herself by collapsing into Weil, by refusing food? Is that not what the anorexic does — treat her body as a material upon which she strategically enacts her own anguish, because she is at war with her own life? To break outside the limits of her awkward body? The only thing unique about Weil is that she writ the anguish of *other people* onto her body.

Perhaps me and Kraus, we anorexics, all anorexic girls the world over; perhaps we are asking ourselves the same question that Weil did:

> 'The body is a lever for salvation, but in what way. *What is the right way to use it?*'[77]

The thing that people often don't understand or choose to disregard about anorexia is that the anorexic has no idea her condition is visible. She is debilitated by an acutely painful awareness of being trapped inside her own body but may have no discrete sense of its shape or condition at all: how it appears in the mirror, or how others might read its language in the street. This is not a position of perspectival denial but rather one of absolute disassociation. People speak of anorexia as a cry for help but, swear to God, I had no idea I was even ill until a friend grabbed me by the shoulders and shook me and screamed it in my face. Even then it took me months to admit what had been happening. Call it delusion or whatever you want. It was 5am and very cold. She shook me because she knew; because she was the same, or had been.

For years I thought Kraus had once described anorexia as "something that happens to girls", and so I resented her because I could not understand myself as a girl. Now I can't find that quote anywhere. Maybe the resentment of that barb, indignantly disappeared, still lives in this text. Over and over again Kraus returns to the psychoanalytic and medical conflation of anorexia and 'manipulation' — in which the anorexic's refusal of food becomes 'consciously manipulative'. She starves herself for attention, or to get what she wants; wounding other people by wounding herself. Kraus even draws a comparison to Sartre, by way of the psychiatrist Pierre Janet; that a girl's guttural sob in response to the question *what's wrong* is not about the inability to say what is troubling her, but rather sobs 'precisely in order not to say anything'.[78]

Rarely does Kraus articulate her own anorexia directly. She does not permit us that kind of access. After Africa/Gavin, the long-distance dom that Kraus fucks over the phone and pens erotic-fictive emails to fails to respond for a few weeks: 'right now it is very difficult to eat'.[79] From her diary in the late nineties, in LA: 'staying at my friend Sabina's house last summer, my weight dropped 20 pounds, below a hundred'[80] [...] 'My heart and stomach flip while waiting in the endless gourmet take-out line at Say Cheese on Hyperion. This is the third full day not eating'.[81]   Many of the most visceral insights Kraus offers are descriptions of food:

'[..]tureens of baby peas in mayonnaise. Ten bucks a quarter pound, they're canned. Little bits of foreign cheese displayed on the top shelf like so many sad specimens. English stilton, camembert. From the bodies of imprisoned animals to the air-conditioned case, it's obvious this food was never touched with love or understanding'.[82]

Eating disorders often resist language. They do not lend themselves to direct testimony because words do not readily attach themselves to the ontological condition of trying to get outside yourself. Hornbacher:

'And even when you have spoken, you find your lexicon vastly insufficient: the words lack shape and taste, temperature and weight. Hunger and cold, flesh and bone are commonplace words. I cannot articulate how those four words mean something different to me than perhaps they do to you, how each of these has, in my mouth, strange flavour'.[83]

Words disconnect from their meanings, moorings; they snick apart. They taste different. As if anorexia does something to the brain's language centre. Because we let nothing in, we lack substance to make words out of. Perhaps anorexia is inarticulable precisely *because* it demands that we entirely abdicate from language. By deferring any instinct of self-preservation, are we denying ourselves access to the sleek contours of a phrase that could begin to trace the faltering limits of this glacier? In fact, it's only when we allow food to enter us that eloquence returns. But a hole in language persists.

Hornbacher continues:

> '[...] it is impossible to sufficiently articulate an inarticulate process, a very wordless time. I did not learn to live by words, so I have found myself with few words to describe what happened'.[84]

I did not learn to live by words, as in: words are not what taught me to live. Or: I learned to live absent of words — I survived, for a time, without them. Or even: I taught myself how to live, ie; *I got better* — without words. Words are not what not healed me. Perhaps the anorexic girl sobs not because she is unable to say what is troubling her, or in order not to say anything at all, but because she lacks a language with which to speak.

This morning I had to admit to myself that this writing is beginning to take its toll. My movements are growing sluggish, the walls of my skull are all claggy and hot. My nightly dreams are soaking, byzantine: warrens of plywood squats and abandoned train yards, muffled parties in the distance and anxious sprints just before the inevitable police raid. I wake up pouring with sweat, rub estradiol into my thighs at midday, fuck myself while it dries, pass out. Do the same again tomorrow. I'm spending so much time with Kraus I think it's finally affecting my ability to eat. Sure, writing works best on coffee and no food until late afternoon, but I know the signs. Some splinter inside me wants to love that hollow slip into emotion-as-hyperspace or the quivering lucidity that Kraus describes; that hunger engenders. I knew this might happen if I took disquiet as my subject and drove myself down into it like a screw.

Kraus says that Deleuze got it right when he wrote that anorexia is nothing to do with 'lack'. 'The question is: how to escape predetermination, the mechanical sign of the meal' — and Kraus agrees: 'Anorexia is not evasion of a social gender role; it's not regression. It is an active stance: the rejection of the cynicism that this culture hands us through its food, the creation of an involuted body'.[85] Deleuze's wife was anorexic so Kraus thinks that's enough reason to trust him. Completely unaware of her use of this word, in my diary last summer I described what was happening to my body as 'becoming ambiguated'. I was no longer ill. I haven't been, seriously, for a long time, but whatever reckoning once deferred through lack was defiantly slipping the noose.

For all my desire to disagree with Kraus, I'll admit that her logic follows its own germ of feeling. Because is that not what I'm pursuing? Is that not what this essay is really about: involution, ambiguation, abstruseness, refusal? After half a life of listening I'll defy anyone's conception of me. Kraus may consider the evasion of a social gender role as a passive stance, but here is the problem: I necessarily can't believe that involution doesn't involve lack, regression, or the shirking of a social gender because *I live and am all those things* — privation; second pubescence; the process of changing my social gender and my sex. I suppose I defy Deleuze too. I defy Kraus for enticing me and for making me sick. It pisses me off. I piss myself off. I don't want to be a romantic person: to adopt the tendency Kraus describes of romantic people as '[...] seeing their lives as grids and mazes, unfolding through an erratic but connected set of lines'[86] because Kraus is one of these people. Simone and Acker too. Romanticising your problems with no intention of fixing them is for people who can afford it, whose problems do not stem from their class position; who are not actively criminalised or willed into death by the state. And yet still I need to eat. I suppose I want to do both.

At the core of *Aliens'*, Kraus is trying to carve out a poetics of anorexia beyond the singular self — beyond the refusal to eat as a crisis of the individuated body: of the girl and the woman and *her problems with herself*, as if they sprang immaculately from the dignity of her own suffering. In so doing Kraus worked to detach anorexia from the haggard condescension of medical pathology and shunt the discourse into a more nuanced territory, where 'eating might be more and less than it seems'.[87] Weil is a useful ally in this shunting because the ugly, beautiful, cowardly, brave, stupid, genius, martian Simone bestows upon Kraus a theoretical framework for uncoupling anorexia from its relationship to embodiment; offering it precedent, shape and spiritual ballast. And so starvation becomes a morally defensible — even logical — response to the lived conditions of the world as such. It is hunger, not empathy, that whets the knife which cuts Kraus through our long-accreted cultural cynicism to arrive at a hecatomb of suffering.

'The panic of altruism is something like the panic of starvation'.[88]

During one of *Aliens* most impassioned passages, just after intoning the title of the book for the first time, Kraus undergoes a kind of paroxysm of feeling:

> '*Impossible* to drink the coffee without thinking about the Inca labourers who picked it, transported from their villages in cattle trucks to work for fifty cents a day ... *Impossible* to view the paintings at the Frick Museum without thinking about the murdered workers, gunned down outside while protesting child labour ... *Impossible* to admire a $2500 pair of shredded Perry Ellis jeans without thinking about the new South African government's decision to spend its limited AIDS budget on education rather than provide its 1 in 5 infected citizens with AZT [...] *WHO MAKES YOUR LIFE POSSIBLE?* I want to scream'.[89]

Is this altruism? Is it not closer to guilt?

No matter how much I read Kraus' work, Simone; no matter how much time I spend in their company, again and again I fail their test by inevitably slipping back into understanding anorexia solely on an individual level — as the manifestation of a troubled embodiment. Repeatedly I arrive at the feeling that *yes*, Kraus is right, anorexia is not simply a pathology of girlhood or a project of narcissistic vanity or an apathetic suicidal pursuit, it *is* an active stance — I know it has to be about *something else*, something infinitely more revealing, but still I can't help but locate that something else *inside the body*: not in the world or it's cynicism, in christian mysticism or post-structuralist philosophy, and not in any abstract attunement to global violences; shot through as this position is, and as the passage above highlights, with troubling white-saviour complexes.

I suppose I fail their test because I am transsexual; because the simple fact of my being reveals the immense privilege bound up in the premise that *the body itself is not the problem*, but also because, quite frankly, I don't buy it.

If, as Kraus says, the world is fucked and uncaring, and if food is a product of the world, meaning that food itself is indivisible from suffering and cynicism, and so in rejecting food we are rejecting any culpability in the world altogether — if we seek to transcend its uncaringness and fuckedness, to not be part of it, to refuse, to say no; then it is in this way that Kraus reinforces the very same contradictions Weil's life was plagued with.

To occupy an individuated body wracked by its own isolation in an uncaring world is not a position of empathy, or one of selflessness. Even less so is the aggressive defence of that body's boundaries, in which nothing, even food, is let in — therefore assuring its continued sovereignty and eventual asphyxiation. Doesn't Kraus say *emotion is a country*, presumably with its own borders? Does she not own property? She purports the same diffuse, self-lacerating extension outside of herself through starvation that Simone does, but the lapses are the same. Is Kraus not white, rich, cis, a homeowner, a landlord and filmmaker, but more importantly — one who does not need to work? A deeply uncharitable part of me is happy to argue that, in response to the relative ease of their material conditions, both Kraus and Weil each projected an absolutely abstracted idea of global suffering into themselves as a caveat for the hyper-individuation and pursuant loneliness that came from their respective class positions; from their inability to connect with other people. There is such voyeurism at work in collapsing any distance between *who you are and what you see*. But disquiet runs deeper than that. Deeper than hunger and negation, than womanhood; it's slippages. It is not possible to know these people — it's not possible to really know anyone. Especially through writing. Simone, Chris, Kathy.

It's hard enough to know yourself.

MATINEE FOR SEVEN PEOPLE & A CEILING CAVING IN

ROLE(S)

ANDROMACHE of Phrygia, the wife of HECTOR,
        daughter of Dymas and Euonë

HECTOR, husband of ANDROMACHE

ACHILLES, leader of the Myrmidons — played by
        Alan Bates, reprising his role as Crossley
        from the 1978 film *The Shout*

SAINT NECTAN of Hartland, son of King Brychan of
        Brycheiniog — played by 20th century
        French philosopher and mystic Simone Weil

JERZY SKOLIMOWSKI, acclaimed Polish film
        director, screenwriter — played by himself

THE FOLLY, Or Fake Ruin

ATHENA, goddess of war — played by Liv Tyler,
        reprising her role of Corey Mason from the
        1995 film *Empire Records*

CHORUS

FOXGLOVES, a trail of innumerable flowers that
            spring up behind St. Nectan as his severed
            head spills blood

THE SEA

PART ONE

PART TWO

129

vi).   *The Balm*

(SAINT NECTAN'S song featuring

FOXGLOVES aria, to the tune of *Just*

(After Song of Songs) by David Lang

and Trio Mediæval)

A HOLE IN THE GROUND / FROM
WHICH THINGS SPILL OUT

It is evening. ANDROMACHE and JERZY SKOLIMOWSKI stand on the balcony of the royal palace of Troy, the seat of HECTOR'S power. JERZY chain-smokes rolled cigarettes, one after another. He fingers a metal cigarette case in his jacket pocket as the cherries wink in and out. Together they gaze over the walls of Troy, and beyond: the columns of black smog that rise from the battlefield — ongoing for three days now. The wind picks up. Banners snap in the frigid breeze.

ANDROMACHE\

> He has been gone so long
>
> husband of mine
>
> into the tracts and fissures, the
>
> scud of war, its mire
>
> to defend shining Troy
>
> from the blood-washed greaves of the Achaeans
>
> O Jerzy, when will he return?
>
> He has been gone so long
>
> husband of Mine
>
> through the tracts and fissures of war he walks
>
> Mighty Hector

SKOLIMOWSKI\

I hate to tell you A but He's not coming back

he's dead as a dodo.

Mighty Hector was ravenous in life

turkey-hungry,

chicken-free,

beside the warm hearth

and flowing breast of Troy; of you, his wife

But he is not coming back

I have seen it

in the oracle of the camera's eye

in the uninterruptible momentum of

cinematic production

he is not coming back,

massive Hector

A\

To place on the fire a large tripod, preparing

a hot bath for Hector, returning from battle

I will do this

I will split the wood and spark the fire

will heave the water and simmer it

perfume the broil with lavender

and coax the soft embers

I will do this

for Big Hungry Hector

who will be weary and gore smeared

who will be carrying his mighty spear

I will tend to the flames

for Ravenous Hector

S\

You seem to shirk

the determinations of storyboarding

or give credence to this

production schedule, ANDROMACHE

much cash is bound up in it

and blood only rolls downhill.

So stoke hope at your own liability

shining ANDROMACHE

feed desire at your own peril

in the trammelled face of loss

pining ANDROMACHE

for Hector has already clasped supplicant knees

has already been laid low

by Achilles' terrible sword

I have seen it

he has already been struck down

into the gore-reeking mud, our

Gorgeous Hector

he walks no longer

as the high Olympians have decreed it

A\

To mix in the cup, preparing three parts

of honey, wine and water

I will do this

for Gorgeous Hector's renewal

I will mix the honeyed wine and water

and attend to the blending

for bright Hector's relief

will pour a small libation in the divot

between the flagstones

under our marital bed

only the finest honey and sweetest wine the

purest water from the coldest stream

I will do this

here in shining Troy

I will do this

I will do this

for Eternal Hector I will

mix the honeyed wine and water

under our marital bed

S\

ANDROMACHE,

woman

you are stubborn

how can the wool be pulled

down over your eyes so far?

Eternal Hector will not be thirsty

he will not be Eternal, even

for his black blood runs thick,

already wetting the ground

amid the mire and rut

from a great sword sinking home its full length,

straight through the neck and breastbone

O,

Achilles' terrible sword

Hector's black blood runs thick.

While you mix honeyed wine

only the waters of the Styx will slake his thirst

under the weight of

Achilles' abominable sword

our Headless Hector

O, ANDROMACHE

blood only runs downhill!

A\

To poor oil from the amphora, preparing

a massage for Fearful Hector, returning

from battle

all golden and languid

I will do this

to ease his weary muscles

to slick his shining calves and cleanse

their graft, from the strife of war

from the weight of the spear

from the shattered shield

I will do this

O,

I will do this for Golden Hector, returning from

battle

oil rolls both ways Jerzy, about the calves

of Golden Hector, returning from battle

O,

oil rolls both ways

S\

ANDROMACHE,

Shining Noble ANDROMACHE,

the deed is already done

He is not coming home

A\

Jerzy,

Despondent Jerzy, my darling

no course is immutable

he will

I know

find his way

back

to me

S\

o,

ANDROMACHE,

I will not dignify this with a response

ARMATURE OR

Later that evening. ANDROMACHE retreats to the cliff overlooking Troy and the battle fuming at its outskirts. As she climbs, she watches the fires burn and the blue limpidity of the sea far away. She has been weeping. At its summit, she throws herself upon the mute ruin of THE FOLLY. Its spindly frame casts a long shadow, low under the beginnings of a bright moon, back down the route she has just walked. Fraying and exhausted, ANDROMACHE slumps against THE FOLLY's collapsed exterior wall. She strokes its stone.

ANDROMACHE\

    Here sweet Folly

    my auxiliary. You called to me

    over the crest of the hill, its LIMIT

    Here broken Folly, my busted surrogate

    my brickening – bowed under the

    weight of DREAD

    for Hector's broken body

    though I am sure it is renewed, surely

    DREAD, sweet Folly

    for Hector's broken body

    I have

FOLLY\

A\

Here lonely Folly

draped about your ramparts I hold out my

SHAPE

dripping

and wantingly

My dear impassive Folly

so silent and wan

Hold under me, some ballast

picked between your stones I strung up my

HAIR

wet

and thickly

My dearest Folly, silent

so hollow and cold

My sister.

Your friable stones linger under the

passage of

YEARS

so braced, for this anxious wreck

can you assure his renewal against the

YEARS?

the reeling YEARS

can you assure Hector's broken body

against the YEARS?

F\

```
/////////////////////////////////////
/////////////////////////////////////
/////////////////////////////////////
/////////////////////////////////////
/////////////////////////////////////
/////////////////////////////////////
/////////////////////////////////////
/////////////////////////////////////
/////////////////////////////////////
/////////////////////////////////////
/////////////////////////////////////
/////////////////////////////////////
/////////////////////////////////////
/////////////////////////,, no ,,,,/////////
/////////////////////////////////////
/////////////////////////////////////
/////////////////////////////////////
/////////////////////////////////////
/////////////////////////////////////
/////////////////////////////////////
/////////////////////////////////////
/////////////////////////////////////
/////////////////////////////////////
/////////////////////////////////////
/////////////////////////////////////
/////////////////////////////////////
/////////////////////////////////////
```

A\

Why   not?

Folly, in our mingling,

in the confluence of missing PARTS

I built myself from you

little ruins,

I built myself from you

little ruins,

and Hector too.

We build ourselves from you

Bright shining Hector too   please

assure Hector's renewal, against the SWORD

decrepit Folly,

the terrible SWORD

Can you assure Victorious Hector's body

against the SWORD?

F\

,,,I cannot ,,

A\

Why   not?

in our substitution, Folly

in the SONG of not being enough, alone

I steady myself against you

little wreck,

I leverage all this through you

little wreck,

and Hector too

we steady each other against you

Dark Brooding Hector too.

Please assure Hector's might

his anguished SPEAR

brittle Folly

his dreadful SPEAR

will you guide Hector's mighty arm

flourishing the SPEAR?

F\

A\

Okay   so

the silent treatment now that's great

You, Folly — my PROXY

who has outlived the whole world; your full

stop

you, PROXY of my body

who has been whittled by the coarse wind into

something impregnable

Cannot pass on the boon of

imperviousness

to my husband, dewy Hector

or guide his SPEAR into the breastbone of

Achilles

Cannot invoke his bloodlust

or still my DREAD

Or will not?

You, Folly — my AUGMENT

who lies about your own position in time

You, AUGMENT of my body

who, fake-ruin, was built to be something

collapsed already

cannot do this

why   not!

Just bring him home on a golden berth, Folly

unbroken

that is all I ask

just let him not be maimed, ruin

un-amputated

that is all I wish

pleas   e

F\

//
//
//
//
//
//
//
//
//
//
//
//
//

```
/////////////////////////////////
/////////////////////////////////
/////////////////////////////////
/////////////////////////////////
/////////////////////////////////
/////////////////////////////////
/////////////////////////////////
/////////////////////////////////
/////////////////////////////////
/////////////////////////////////
/////,heisirreperablygoneANDROMACHE
hewillnotbecomingback,,,////////////////
/////////////////////////////////
/////////////////////////////////
/////////////////////////////////
/////////////////////////////////
/////////////////////////////////
/////////////////////////////////
/////////////////////////////////
/////////////////////////////////
/////////////////////////////////
/////////////////////////////////
/////////////////////////////////
/////////////////////////////////
/////////////////////////////////
/////////////////////////////////
/////////////////////////////////
/////////////////////////////////
/////////////////////////////////
/////////////////////////////////
/////////////////////////////////
/////////////////////////////////
/////////////////////////////////
/////////////////////////////////
/////////////////////////////////
/////////////////////////////////
/////////////////////////////////
/////////////////////////////////
/////////////////////////////////
/////////////////////////////////
/////////////////////////////////
/////////////////////////////////
```

```
//////////////////////////////////////
//////////////////////////////////////
//////////////////////////////////////
//////////////////////////////////////
//////////////////////////////////////
//////////////////////////////////////
//////////////////////////////////////
//////////////////////////////////////
//////////////////////////////////////
//////////////////////////////////////
//////////////////////////////////////
//////////////////////////////////////
//////////////////////////////////////
//////////////////////////////////////
//////////////////////////////////////
//////////////////////////////////////
//////////////////////////////////////
//////////////////////////////////////
//////////////////////////////////////
//////////////////////////////////////
//////////////////////////////////////
//////////////////////////////////////
//////////////////////////////////////
//////////////////////////////////////
//////////////////////////////////////
//////////////////////////////////////
//////////////////////////////////////
//////////////////////////////////////
//////////////////////////////////////
//////////////////////////////////////
//////////////////////////////////////
//////////////////////////////////////
//////////////////////////////////////
//////////////////////////////////////
//////////////////////////////////////
//////////////////////////////////////
//////////////////////////////////////
//////////////////////////////////////
//////////////////,,i'msorry,,,,//////////////
//////////////////////////////////////
//////////////////////////////////////
//////////////////////////////////////
//////////////////////////////////////
//////////////////////////////////////
//////////////////////////////////////
//////////////////////////////////////
```

A\

oh	Christ	PROXY
ARMATURE		SWORD
HAIR		SPEAR
SONG		SHAPE
YEARS		LIMIT
DREAD		FOLLY

In the immortal words of Elizabeth Fraser:

I do not accept it

who'll ever win?

Gee,

you're just

so ephemeral

go back for new

for new

in vain,

it

failed

F\

GIBBETED CLAY

Daybreak. It is very cold. Down in the churning field of war, before the gates of Troy, fires burn innumerable. ACHILLES stands poised over a supplicant HECTOR, mortally wounded and squirming in the black mud. His mighty spear lies shattered about their sandaled feet. Lingering in the background, JERZY SKOLIMOWSKI sits mute and brooding in his director's chair. The banners which previously lashed in the breeze now hang still. LIV TYLER, taking the form of a crested owl, surveys the scene from a rocky outcrop on high. ACHILLES / ALAN BATES leans in. Steam pours from his heaving chest, and vents in plumes from his mouth and nose as he speaks haltingly — utterly spent. He raises his sword.

ACHILLES\

It is done,

Hector

I feel the long arch of your

nails clutching at the back of my knees

the cinders at the back of your eyes

the crumpled boss of your shield

they are each .

winking out and

like this city, you are

broken innumerably, sweet boy.

Troy will be laid

to waste and

picked into splinters, its women

thrown over the shoulder,

its children

lashed into the sea

while the noble Achaean's,

with their golden carves,

will tear into its white meat

into what tastes best,

as the high Olympians have

decreed it.

You have done well,

as Hector

playing mighty shining Hector,

leader of men, you've played him well,

Big Hungry Hector,

but no longer.

No bath awaits

you or perfumed house;

honeyed hands

the slick of oil, tangy sage;

no sweet wine or its

fringing glow.

I do not even wish for you good

lodgings in Hades.

May the dogs lick your wounds with their

scouring tongues

and bring pestilence forth in reams

a sundry for your infractions against

the Gods,

and against your people,

and against myself

which will never be enough.

All this for Patroclus, I have done it

I have done it all for Patroclus.

Hector, it is done.

Kneel

for now, you know

what comes next.

HECTOR/

Christ my side

I am spil l

[   ] am s pilling   out

My N A M E   .   ,

Hector

It is min e

ALAN,

you canno t

un   ma   ke that

This name is mine

A nd like you said!

I-I've held it

close

played it

better than anyo ne

else

hhh h FUC k

it i s M E

I , i [   ] mean

[   ]

will spit on your feet

claw deep into the sinew

Achille s

at the back of your k nees

If you think

that any harrowed blad e can sunder

the fra me and the moniker

th e house and the home

you dare ask me to

take you kindly ?

[   ] won't de   base myself in

that lateral po ol of mercy ALAN

[   ] am irreparably bound

u p in

i T

ACHILLES raises his sword. Smoking noncommittally, JERZY SKOLIMOWSKI eyes the scene as it shudders back and forth. A gentle drizzle starts falling. The cherries of his cigarettes, one after another, pick out his harsh visage intermittently. As he flicks his ash, JERZY notices that it doesn't float slowly to the ground but begins streaming upward, past his outstretched nose. The grey drizzle has begun to do the same: sifting into the sky as if everything were upside down. His chair tremors and he feels damp under his chin. Something breaks. A white thunderclap.

SKOLIMOWSKI/

ALAN!

christ

ACHILLES,

DO it now!

s hit

End it NO W!

ACHILLES sword falls, arcing through HECTOR's outstretched neck with a single stroke. Lightning cracks across the firmament in a shrieking flash. Black blood is thrown into the air, but does not fall, and instead begins to trickle into the sky like silk, mingling with the ash from JERZY's cigarettes. HECTOR slumps into the muck, dead. ATHENA eyes ACHILLES for a few more seconds until he falls to his knees, in tears. Then she flies away.

OWL, MY LINGER

Then, miraculously, New York. ATHENA/LIV TYLER sits in the back of a cab. She is rifling through her notebooks which are individually pinned to her bronze and burnished armour. Each book is scabbed at the edges with livid red wax seals — they rustle as the cab goes over each hole in the broken tarmac. She is exasperated, blood stained.

ATHENA/

God, the corpses

all this stupid mess

I guess it'd be nice if you didn't hate my guts, boys

— now where is it?

I know I put it somewhere

1 2 3

Urgh

the gore and slick

they can squabble like children

see if I give a shit — there it is

'Mystic quadruple zero zero'

I wrote this poem for Nancy Holt:

4 5 6

{a*hem*}

"Two bodies eventually

only one body   *one*

plane crash one poem one dedication   *two*

people   *two*

continents   *one*

wood that is one part of a pair so one of   *two*

really one photograph   *one*

boot two boulders one million dalliances of dappled

sunlight   *five*

poems eventually only one poem — here the first   *one*

only   *one*

for one partner three for three friends one for   *one*

murderer (acquitted)   *one*

example of well preserved oak woodland (pedunculate)

the second in

Northern Ireland   *five*

spades five maps five divined evocations   *five*

lies which are simply not telling the truth for a time

which I guess is   *one*

type of dishonesty you know   *one*

type of interiority   *ten*

billion barrels of crude oil

four tunnels one sun two lives and then one life and

then one life again but in the singular

sense this time really one present body   *one*

absent body   *innumerable*

orange dots twenty inkjet prints *one hundred*

and twenty six format

transparencies *two*

core themes the agency of testimony & the nature of the

gift mystic   *zero*

zero zero zero *twelve*

D's you know I really

can't

find

it."

I guess it's alright

I guess she, well

the diet pills, *The The*

"you didn't get up this morning because

you didn't go to bed" — and everything else

I guess Corey'll wear a slipped mini skirt and

the little blue blouse, to shoplift

For what, for Achilles? For the rush?

For love? Shit

inculcate me sweetly, green tartan

sublimate her into

~my sugared fist~

O, Hector

1 2 3

hash brownies & eros

the whites of your eyes

4 5 6

slip it into my golden palm quick

I'll see all your spears spurned, in time

dashed in the tide, to rust

and burnish in the broil

~my wet hot mess~

spit it all out and slip the gist

LOVE IS A MANY-HEADED HEDONIST

Dusk. ANDROMACHE, after fleeing the FOLLY's outcrop the night before, finds herself lost amidst the cold mire where the battle once raged. She has been running for a day and a night, and has no sense of her whereabouts. It is completely silent except for the flapping of torn banners in the wind. There is smoke; smouldering corpses; thick blood in deep ruts across the churned soil. The rigging of the Achaeans black ships sit morbidly in the far distance like a row of rotten teeth. Through the mist, she makes out ATHENA, holding her helmet to her breast. She is standing over the headless body of Hector and slowly pouring wine onto his severed neck from a golden cup.

ANDROMACHE/

    So that's it then

ATHENA/

    That's it

A/

    Nothing left to do

A/

    Nothing left

A/

I'm left with nothing

A/

Try not to worry about it

A/

What else could I have done

A/

Nothing,

there was nothing you could do

A/

You did not protect him?

You guided the sword?

A/

I did not protect him,   I guided the sword

A/

Now you'll pour libation

A/

Now I'll pour libation

A/

And I'll mourn him

A/

Do not mourn him

A/

Okay then

A/

Okay then

okay

THE BALM

Nighttime. On a single cliff overlapping the very edge of what is perceivable, ST. NECTAN / SIMONE WEIL stands surveying the corpulent black glass of THE SEA; the white foam and the crests of the waves where the light pricks. The wind is high and all is soft under a thin rime of salt. Blood leaks slowly from a very deep wound in her neck, but she is unperturbed: strolling across the low grass of the cliff top, picking between the sheep as they sleep — the cold stars cowled over everything. Where the blood drips, spools of FOXGLOVES unfurl and bloom. They begin to sing with each step ST. NECTAN takes. She clasps a small silver bell in her left hand, which she rings.

ST NECTAN/

    Here I go, O

    back up the old tack

    an arrogant flick of the tail and

    two sharp knives that's

    all it took

    that's all the mercy shown me

    I must find my moonlight pool of grace

    tonight, little bell:

    my moonlit pool of grace

it dances so deeply in the night's slick

I must get back to it

to wash myself

to cleanse the sawing wound

of decreation at my nape

under silver water; that moonlit pool

it's glassy and cold

little bell

take me back to it

Grace,

All grace

I cannot give in to it —

to that collapse

into hunger and its unmaking

Soft lilt of my silver bell

clap, please! Ring me assuredly

toward my pool

like quicksilver

let silver seawater flood me

pour through my nose, my ears

my mouth down my

throat through the corners of my eyes

let me be suspended in it

Thats how I'll feel you —

I'll empty myself up, out

for you little bell; lead me

into my moonlit pool of grace tonight

so glassy and cold

please little bell

that's where I'm headed

      Grace,

      All grace

FOXGLOVES/

   ...

   {RECURSIVE}

   ...

{VERMILLION}

...

{ABLATED}

...

{CONSOLED}

...

SN/

Little flowers: Hector is dead, and

this slice out my neck, each siblings of collapse

a catastrophe of a king

a caricature of a beautiful girl

I'm sick of it, the act

all dried up

{a saint doesn't rouge his lips but he could

a king doesn't lose his name but he does}

Through force and poison

the whole world runs

on force and poison! Little bell

take me back to my moonlit pool

for grace and silver, it's gravity

I'll make the ash and blood pour upward

{a house doesn't dig a hole but it could

a home doesn't learn its name but it does}

Grace,

All grace. For grace and silver

Slowly, let it seep into the perforations

of my skinning

stitch my head aloft

back onto its shoulders, because

O, Gravity

the sea is dark and deep

You are silver and stitching but

THE SEA is endless, and sexy

all pulp black wash and rush

salty flecks of foam about the mouth

So dark and deep; little bell

I must drink it

F/

    ....

    {RECURSIVE}

    ...

    {VERMILLION}

    ...

    {ABLATED}

    ...

    {CONSOLED}

    ...

SN/

Little bell; listen close

if I don't make it they'll

erect a small well for me in the woods

deep in the woods

where bluebells, wild garlic spit

beneath a rotten steel grate

And a glass-framed photograph

of my visage will sit atop it,

a little stone well deep in the woods

and people will drink from it

little bell; so gracefully

so gratefully

Because your tinkling will draw them in

as it does me; toward THE SEA

your clasp and clapper

and they will drink the moonlit pool of grace

as they go, too

so let me go, release me

from altruism — it's crisis

from cynicism — little bell

from the spite of the world

O, I will drink it

THE SEA, cold silver; throw it back

down through the long distance of the years

To hold him

To hold his hand

And shake him

Grace,

All grace

For grace and silver

O, little bell;

the girl I could have been!

F/

...

{RECURSIVE}

...

{VERMILLION}

...

{ABLATED}

...

{CONSOLED}

...

JUST MY SONG

JUST MY BELOVED

JUST MY HANDS

JUST YOUR EYES

JUST MY WOUND

JUST MY BREAST

JUST OUR VINEYARD

AND MY PRIDE

JUST YOUR BED

JUST YOUR SHEETS

JUST YOUR PAIN

JUST YOUR MILK

JUST MY GARMENT

JUST YOUR LIPS

JUST YOUR BONES

AND MY APPEARANCE

AND MY GARDEN

JUST YOUR FLOCK

JUST YOUR TEETH

JUST YOUR FANCY

JUST YOUR FEET

JUST YOUR TWO BREASTS

JUST YOUR NECK

AND YOUR HUNGER

AND YOUR BREATH

{OH SISTER}

JUST YOUR LOSS

AND MY COAT

JUST YOUR WALK

JUST YOUR THIGHS

JUST MY BREATH

JUST MY HOLDING

AND MY LOVE

JUST YOUR SONG

JUST MY LOVE

JUST MY HOLDING

JUST MY BED

JUST YOUR SLEEP

JUST YOUR DREAMS

AND MY FEAR

AND MY THIGHS

AND YOUR HANDS

{OHHHHHHHH SISTERRRRRRRRR}

JUST YOUR CITY

JUST YOUR SPIT

JUST YOUR HISTORY

JUST YOUR GARDEN

JUST YOUR BODY

JUST YOUR ORGANS

JUST YOUR TEETH

AND MY BODY

AND MY TWO BREASTS.

AND MY MOTHER'S HANDS

AND MY HAIR

AND YOUR STONES

AND YOUR VOICE

AND MY BELONGING

AND MY VINEYARD

JUST YOUR LEFT HAND

JUST YOUR RIGHT HAND

AND MY FATHER'S EYES

AND YOUR BELOVED

AND YOUR YEARS

AND MY FAMILY

AND MY SELF

AND M Y   SELF

AND M   Y   SE LF

ST NECTAN / SIMONE stands on the shore. It is midnight. She rings the silver bell once, its cold trill bouncing off the dormant cliffs, and finds no answer. She slips the bell into a small pocket in her trousers and walks through the basalt sand into the glassy water. The innumerable FOXGLOVES, fully ripe now and lurid pink, have completed their aria. They trail behind SIMONE; entering the sea in her wake. Their petals detach one by one and drift errantly to the surface, like moths. Then she disappears.

{CURTAIN}

4~

REQUIA

Hi, hello, I am writing to you.

It is mid morning and I am writing to you. I am lying in bed. You are sitting somewhere atop a style at the edge of a green field or down at the water's edge maybe. By the quay. You are probably adrift on the stones watching the waves lap in, deep in thought. You sitting there and me lying in bed.

There are so many more important things I could be doing in this moment, with this time that I am taking to write to you, while you squat there at the water's edge. Time; so often taken but rarely given. I want to give you the time. *The* time — something useful. To *do* with, to *be done* with. What else could I be doing with this time, the time that apparently I have so much of in this moment, for the first time in a long time, lying in bed? I could be emailing my doctor I suppose, I could be emailing my fake doctor who I've never seen to lie to him. I could be emailing lovers, too, and friends, as I lie here. I could be painting lipstick on my tits and signing a letter by pressing them against the envelope and posting it off to someone who might expect it and still others who might not. I could be writing small notes and posting them through the crack of a draughty window in this dilapidated old schoolhouse in the East Midlands where wisteria is growing through the window into the room where I am lying, taking over the ceiling — but still it is February and so it is brown and not lilac. Dudley calls it the semi-mythical house of a million things in which five hundred thousand of those things are broken and I love that. Might you? The notes could say short nonsenses like, 'vivacious antediluvian alacrity' or 'grotesque orchard abundant livid tracheotomy' because I like to see words move fundamentally in their own little cellular units. They might mouth small platitudes like 'hello gorgeous' or 'liquid eyeliner NOT pencil' or 'bleached eyebrows are out' or 'get better at crying' or 'I'll do what's right for both of us' or 'reply to Alice' or 'rest is fundamental' or 'feminine, feminine, feminine'. They could even be short, fortifying quotes from people I love, like 'You are going along with yourself' or 'Thank you for being my friend' or 'The essay as an exercise in digging-one's-heels-in' or 'Throw a party! Rub one out in the mirror! Get a blood test done for the shits and giggs!' or 'It makes sense that shame knocks on the door of the home that you're building right as the last brick is laid'. But I am not writing these small notes in soft pencil and tearing them off of a larger sheet of paper and posting them through the crack of the draughty window through which wisteria is coiling into this dilapidated old school house in the East Midlands; I am not emailing lovers or painting lipstick on my tits and signing a letter with them or emailing doctors, my fake doctor that I've never seen, to lie to them as a means of survival, I am writing this, I am writing to someone, you, a letter; I am writing to you: that is who I am writing to. You — my I that I no longer know.

What is the way in? How do I get at you? I'll start with how you looked.

You were handsome and people said that about you. You were handsome in that kind of unmediated way men or people who appear to be them are often praised for being. When I say unmediated I suppose I mean to say natural. Naturally handsome. Which is another way of saying still, or singular: handsome in that you represented a stable image of being.

Because you were raised by a working-class single mother who inherited from her mum a contrary blend of reticent timidity — she would always say of her mother, "She wouldn't say boo to a goose" — and rebellious tomboy ebullience that was offset by quintessentially feminine good looks and the advent of punk, you were raised to believe that image management as an aspirational project of class was spiritually indefensible and image management in terms of the physical mediation of your presentation was largely unconscionable. You agreed with the first and the second stuck in you like a splinter. This was the mid-2000s of course, and Jersey Shore, Katie Price, luminous orange skin and french tips were the *par excellence* of femininity in your small working class and partially under-class rural town in coastal North Devon and the rest of England more generally. Early 00's glam had not yet been relegated to the suburbs and hinterlands — where old things cling and new things take a long while to arrive — as it eventually would in the 2010's, before dying out entirely.

Blissfully unaware of this looming redundancy, those girls who were the granddaughters of fishermen, farmers or shipbuilders — and the daughters of people on the dole after the fisheries closed, the shipbuilders shut down, and the farms got priced out — clacked and tottered across the schoolyard. Thick concealer transmuted itself virally between each girl and other surfaces; skin, uniforms, handbags and door handles. Their eyelashes were long, curled and streaked with claggy mascara that collected in clumps; offset by a pink gloss or frosty lipstick. Each girl re-applied herself with an intoxicating medley of deodorants and supermarket perfumes throughout the day until they congealed and hung over her head in a permanent miasma; opulently vanilla and aluminium, literally but not figuratively gagging. It was all very drag. Very major. You don't see it anymore: that particularly literal application of beauty's embedded logos, in which the face isn't considered as a whole but rather each individual aspect — eyes, lips, skin, brows, lashes, cheeks, nose — are treated as separate indices of femininity, until the face takes on a kind of disjointed malengé. And I mourn it, that clumsiness, like a necessary rite, an essential failure; a gorgeous interstitial between the first hormonal eruption and its settling; the recognition that girlhood is not something that you arrive at automatically but that which has to be *worked out:* the painterly, irrepressible maximalism of a poor girl's first flush.

They were your friends, these girls, you were drawn to them. Or girls like them. Girls on a sliding scale of unapologetic glamour from meek to full tilt. And they welcomed you in, or at least tolerated you, because you were still seemingly ambivalent about the whole thing, because you had not yet taken on that stable image of being or worked out how to convincingly appear to have done so. But there was a problem: if the femininity of these girls was 'fake', as your mother, but in fairness culture at large, said — or was modulated by 'fake' things; clip-ins, extensions, nails, lips, eyelashes, tans, cheap, premature, accessible botox, scraped back scalps and those quilted black Paul's Boutique jackets embossed in livid pink — if those hallmarks of girlhood were both totalising and reprehensible, essential and yet fictitious, desirable and yet gaudy, innate and yet cartoonish, because they were not your mother, but the only alternative example of femininity available to you was your mother, who could not be an avatar of what was beautiful, or an introduction to what it meant to be an object of desire, or an education in being both desirable and beautiful as a woman, but in a different way, a third way, because she was your mother — perhaps that is why you found nothing you could relate to.

They were your friends, these girls, as I've said. Something your mother could never be, at least for now — something your father tried to be so desperately. These girls were friendly in that they let you be around them, they let you mill about at the margins of their presence so as to soak up their language; the burgeoning language of their bodies which they were carefully refining to learn how they could relate to one another and also to themselves. Some of them were mean and that was fine. Or at least their friendliness was occasionally shot through with sudden eruptions of meanness or enforced distance. Because of course you were not them, those girls, despite your ambivalence, despite having not yet taking on that stable image of being, and so you could never truly be safe around them just as they could never truly be safe around you. It was a matter of trust. Meanness or it's jag; the periodic revocation of proximity — where you could hang out, who you could eat lunch with, who's cigarettes you could smoke, who you could text under the table, who's jokes you could laugh at — they were tests: tests to see if you snapped, or more accurately to see if you *ceased to be ambivalent*, like a tangled rubber band pulled back and recoiling into the congruence of a ring, into something recognisable, something that has a use, like time, and so time had to be used as a test, as a weapon of trust. How long could you remain separate from their shared warmth, from that heady fugue of acrid perfume and clumsy blush; the sickly balm of their language and lashes? How long could you stand it, to be adrift in the corridors of no-name, without a shared language, stumbling periodically into the hard edges of those who had arrived, already and so effortlessly, at their own language, at stability or a naturally stable image, and who conversely recognised that ambivalence in you immediately; that as-of-yet-unstilled or not-yet-convincingly-performed stillness, and therefore clocked you intuitively, on a primal level — I think it was Fran who told me *your bullies know you best* — as inferior, or at least as un-stilled and therefore innately vulnerable to their hardness, set about hardening their hard edges further, into hard words or hard blows or simply the hard gesture of getting the shit kicked out of you. All this, all that time; those girls used each period of withdrawal as a test to see if you could be trusted, to see if they were safe in your ambivalence, and whether you actually could soak up the language that they expelled and which poured from their skin so generously, in spools — really, to see if you loved them: not romantically or platonically, but rather to see if you were *in love with them*, with them *as girls*, as a collective pronoun, with what it meant to be a girl; because of course no matter the length of time or the abruptness of their revocation of that proximity, no matter how big the distance regularly wedged between you and those girls, it could never be as big or as long as the seemingly permanent distance between you and your mother — because she was already old in your teenage eyes; old enough to have become still, and so was self-evident, fully-formed and naturally beautiful, even if her appellation of femininity was invisible to you because she could not be an object of desire — and so you always came back to those girls, or at least they always let you back in, because of course you could not become still, you never could, it was an impossibility, thereby finally proving that perhaps around you they could be safe.

But of course the one so desiring of safety, who pursued it so keenly and with every air of desperation, although they never expressed it because they did not have the right to ask for that safety, because they were ambivalent, and because they had not yet taken on that stable image of being, even though they were ultimately expected to, was you.

So these girls: they held or tolerated you in the clumsy interstitial of their burgeoning girlhood while you remained stuck in the clumsy interstitial of your own arrested ambivalence. This was only possible for a time. You knew it on some level. Or rather, your body knew it while your brain had no awareness, which is in its own way a kind of knowing, the first one — because your ambivalence became increasingly untenable as puberty began to unilaterally inflict its ravages upon everyone in sight: not just those girls, but the girls and the others, those others with hard edges. Perhaps for this reason you tried so very hard to please them, those girls, desperately, fawningly; those girls who were slowly becoming stilled in their own way but who remained open somehow — more accessible, more achievable. They let you in and they hugged you or they demanded a certain degree of physical proximity to you, you were permitted that kind of access: to their waists in an embrace, to their breasts with your head laid atop their school jumper, or in the summer a white polo, unbuttoned at the top, and even occasionally, in secret, even as you smouldered with shame, even while making eye contact, to cup them gently in your hands; those breasts that were new or were at least coming in. These girls granted you access to their bodies in this way, their already becoming-still bodies that were at once — as you were constantly, piercingly reminded — both beautifully fake and agonisingly real, because they felt safe, but also because they needed you to be near to them so that they could *try proximity out*: to see how it felt to be near a body that was not theirs, that was not another girl's, even though in their embrace you became one, even in name only, or in the realm of language only, silently inside yourself, unconfessed, because still you were smouldering with shame; burning with guilt even as you attained safety by slipping into their bodies momentarily, even as they vibrated with the vigilance and anxiety of being in proximity to a body that was not theirs, despite the fact that it was, despite the fact that really it was you who was safe with them. And maybe they thought you were gay just as your mum had asked you in the kitchen that one time, which you were already maybe, but not in the way that either they or your mother or you knew or could know at the time.

How did you try to please them? You made yourself available. Little things, their problems — you held them. You made yourself available to them just as they had made their language, gradually, and their bodies, momentarily, available to you. These problems felt small but were in fact quite large. Not yet adult problems, but certainly not the problems of a child. These girls, like every girl, they had needs. Their lives were not easy. No girl's life the whole world over is easy, and harder is the life of the woman to come, but the lives of these girls-becoming-women especially. Their lives at home, amongst their families, their lives at school, their new lives at work in cafes, bars or retail; each of these conflicting and overlapping lives — in each of which they were being asked to become a woman, or were being presented with the untenability of remaining a girl, and were thereby forced to become one of three separate women, or rather three women simultaneously; learning, as they would have to, the enforced delineation of desire, femininity and its revocation so as to survive in the world, or at least inhabit it — they were hard.

So you tried to hold these hard things for those girls, their lives, their burgeoning problems. They came to you with them: a fight with one girl, a girl stealing another's boyfriend, an abusive boyfriend or parent, an abusive ex-boyfriend or step-parent, a friend that was in hospital, a friend that was suicidal, a friend that had successfully taken her own life, a grandmother wracked with cancer, a dog hit by a car, a first period or a late period, a pregnancy, an abortion, a brother in prison, exams and mothers, popped-cherries and bailiffs; you worked to hold them. You gripped each problem so tightly because you thought they might be lumps of coal that could be squeezed into diamonds. But this was impossible, no matter how hard you gripped them, because these were children's problems teetering at the margins of adulthood, meaning that they were unresponsive to the gripping of another child because they were unwieldy and modulated by bigger forces, adult forces: infrastructure, addiction, healthcare, policing, incarceration, landlordism, austerity, bigotry, nationalism — and so just as these problems could so easily slip into the austere gravity of the adult world they could just as easily regress into the hysteria of the child's. You were caught, or really you put yourself between these two positions; between graveness and hysteria, between adulthood and childhood, in your ambivalence, but still you held tight. You gripped those lumps of coal, those lumps of coal that could not become diamonds, and you squeezed them until you lacerated yourself upon their blunt edge. You took them inside you and hewed them into your body. The moment you became aware of these problems they became yours; there was no other conclusion to draw. You and those girls, you shared the same language now, or at least you were learning the language that they were learning, so as to relate to one another and also to themselves, but their language could not be related to you, or really it was defined by your inability to access it — because you were unspeakable in it, there was not a word for you, even as you were adrift in it, so the words just bounced off, or got snuffed out, and you felt the loss of that shared language keenly. In the collapse of coherence that followed — in language, in your physicality — there opened up a hole which you tried to stuff shut with these problems, those lumps of coal that had become, or which you'd made, yours to squeeze: problems spoken in a girl's burgeoning language to speak her burgeoning girlhood, your absence of it, your ambivalence, their ambivalence towards you, and in that stuffing-shut stave off a reckoning that could have come much sooner had it not been for such a colossal exertion of pressure.

You held these problems because your mother had you hold hers. You loved her. Or maybe it would be more accurate to say there was no one else to hold them, spatially speaking. You loved her. Spatially speaking you were two people in one house with only absence around and they were tumbling out, your mother's problems, her lumps of coal; they were proliferating and lacerating and they slipped her grasp because there were simply too many to hold — even in her strong, dextrous copper hands — and they spilled out onto the floor in sooty piles. She shovelled spades of them into the stove after dad left. There was no other fuel. But they did not burn clean.

These problems, your mother's problems, unlike the problems of those girls, they did not teeter between the world of the adult and the world of the child because they were resolutely *of the woman.* By which I mean to say they were not immediately apprehendable to the mind of a child. They had no clear anchor in the YA novels or TV dramas you used to articulate those girl's problems; those problems with which you learnt about narrative, so as to turn them over in your hand and scrutinise each one for a fix. These were the problems of a grown woman: nebulous and murky, long, calcified and darkly shimmering. Their mechanisms were shrouded by a kind of baroque obtuseness that was entirely inaccessible to your ambivalent I. Their intelligence, or rather the way in which they *thought,* these problems, those lumps of coal, *what their rationale was* — was not the kinetic cause and effect immediately apprehendable to a child, but rather the Gordian logic of sublimated emotions beyond your purview; emotions of a scale so remote and a trajectory so arcane that they might as well have emerged not from your mother but from outside of time altogether, or the moon. Also things were hidden from you. Or at least, their being-hidden was revealed to you in their eventual revelation as things that had been hidden, when they were revealed, all too abruptly, as things that had happened. You were shown their evidence prematurely in a spasm of desperation or a desire for understanding, and so upon being made witness to them their architecture was immediately, necessarily absurd, in that you could not understand their evidence, because their status *as evidence* was dependent on a set of relations that you could not possibly have access to — because they were an adult's lump of coal, not a child's — and so the impressions they left were not so much malignant but rather entirely opaque.

What else did you do? You started drinking. You tried to smoke, or at least tried to develop the affect of having smoked, or of being a smoker. Which, in your relative naivety and inevitable rural sequestering from the world at large you imagined to be a kind of aloof detachment anchored in the gesture of the held cigarette and its glowing nib, as well as your place among the circle of girls who were also smoking; who were repeating those same conceited gestures by watching one another repeat them, in this circle which was a ring, something coherent, if only for a moment, in someone else's garden, despite the fact that the ring would soon break apart and despite the fact that none of you really did. Smoke I mean. Also, you tried to have sex. And in those earliest forays you immediately brushed up against a ragged disjunct between the ways in which your body was desired and your ability to recognise it as desirable as such. This is because you had no notion of its shape. When one of these girls expressed their desire of you, for you, to you, it was not clear whether they were joking or if the whole thing was a prank. In fact, the exact way that it was communicated was so sudden, wasn't it? Out here, in the park, right in the open, so abruptly, so unexpectedly, with no one else around. Who else could it be? Which meant that it was clearly directed at you, or at least desire was being dangled in front of you, to see if you took the bait, because how could they desire you? You, who was ambivalent, who was already becoming half-them, those girls, fleetingly, flickeringly; guttering momentarily into girlhood in those rare moments that they came so close to you, as they were doing now, and wouldn't that mean that they desired themselves? Which you knew was an impossibility because you'd never seen it. So surely those other girls were hiding in the bushes, weren't they? Ready to spring out and run towards you both — you and this girl who had drawn the short straw or been dared into this dangling of desire in front of an ambivalent non-girl who was necessarily already a small part of themselves — to laugh and to cry with laughing until you ran off or an adult appeared or the whole spectacle just collapsed in on itself. But still the desire was real. Or at least curious. The first time one of those girls pulled your foreskin back with her mouth, her teeth aglint in a brigade of wire braces, you thought that something had broken. Did you enjoy it? I don't know. But there was something in having your body so lividly revealed to you.

And then what? The endocrine system took hold and the lumps and bruises and the hard words and the birthdays and the shaved head and it all just got wrought into place.

You, my I that I longer know, my I that was once me, what did you do then; during that time when our I's were one, after you relinquished ambivalence — when we were twins for a time, seemingly seamlessly the same? Maybe it's time for you to write to me. Our mother lost a girl late-term a few years before us, she could have been our sister. I think she wanted to call her Verity, or Violet. I know it began with V. I wonder sometimes whether she remained in me, V, or some germ of me was already available in her, to eventually be adrift in the miscarriage of you — in which I let you go; this I, me, who is now writing to you, the I who split you in half.

Some time in 2017 you wrote this:

> "two doors open
> we have arrived where we are
> passion-flower airsoup
> clogs our breath
>
> i step off the loading bay

you step off the loading bay

we are up to our shoulders in vines and steely

grasses

in the old country there was a vine called *wait*

n see

it had talons that curved and were two or three

inches long

why did they call it wait n see

? i ask

they called it wait n see

because if you were caught in them

their talons would sinkhook

into you

and you could not move

without making bigger

tears in

your   self

and eventually you'd get stuck

and bleed out

then your body, as it fell apart

would feed the roots

below at the base of the tree

you say

i say *fuck*

you say *don't worry*

they have been extinct for a long time

except in your head you know that extinct is
the wrong word
and that they evolved into the flowers
hanging above us

now they are pollinated by flying lizards
who do not run so hot
whose insides aren't steaming but
are more like a reservoir at night
still;

stamen became of their talons

hmph- crumpled brow like an ordinance map
i unsheathe the vi-blade at my waist
and begin slicing through the undergrowth

the plants are hot and moist
and the blade hums softly
the hum travels up my arm
it makes my arm fuzzy
my bones and layers of muscle
      sinew tendon water fat
are singing in tune

your Gosha Rubchinskiy spider-silk double
breasted suit jacket
reflector field enabled
begins to rip and tear among the branches
tiny lesions
no matter

you say
small gashes in the mirror of your torso
suck in the light

languid pink motes
lap at the edges of my hands
as i raise them to the waxing suns
so that the symbols on my palms engolden,
from inside
lancing a brassy beacon outward;
a fleshy compass blooming and
softly embossed
to light up the path ahead with
arrows whirling, then steadily
caustic warmth leaks in
under the *skyn*

i sweat under my Marithe Francois Girbaud
crystal sheaf bodysuit
you sweat too
i see it beading at the edge of your eye

we can smell each other

{beyond is as much a place
as before
yet we are going into
not exiting}

we make camp
a fire glows
and listen to *Copenhagen* by Scott Walker
and *Square Toed Leather Boot* by Quay Dash

small things scurry in the undergrowth
sextuplet-eyes catch the light

insulator foil collapses outward
covering us

satellites   *twizt*

        as they fall out of

        the

            sky

in the brittle morning air you draw a new
machine
with soft tools; a plastic web hewn in reverse
you pick it up
and carry it into the shrub

i can hear it talking to you, the machine
as you walk away

i strap a white kitsune mask
onto my face
the silk chords intwine with my fingers
in a rustling skip

the mask depicts a fox with the wry smile
of something that can change
i stroke the wooden edge of the mask where it
meets my jaw
and follow you

after a time — a huge break
across our path
poorly sutured; deep cloven tract
dragged unwilling through the earth

far below at the bottom
a crystal lattice, shaded from the morning suns
by the deepening of the break

glimmers with intent
and potential

looking down I see you already hopping
between too-big steps cut into the raw stone

{glancing to the back of my eyes i watch,
in the past
as sheet ice grinds its way through the valley,
unheedingly
and soon the
yellow methane sea rolling in
engulfing}

and not for the first time
i wish
i could change

like the fox

the tinny bubbling from your illustrated friend
trip up the steps drunkenly
and trickle into my ears
it is cool now under the mask

still, i follow
still, the gold light leaks from my palm
picking out the ground ahead

swinging in a mad waltz
in time with us

we walk down the steps for a day
or maybe it is thee
i behind my face
you talking to your machine

it is growing now
it has become your arm
it is coiled under your skin at the base of your
shoulder
now your arm talks

{we exchange a word only three or four times
and fuck twice
but your arm wouldn't shut up during
and i couldn't relax
and i didn't like it}

we're really deep in the break now:
down here the syrupy light from above
seeps in less and less
it runs down the breakface for a little
then dries up

we get twisted one night glanding *snapdowse*

rolling around in the dust
and i realise that the light from above is
gradually being replaced
by the broken red glow from below

the crystal lattice is swelling slowly;
from the brink of the break it looked like a
small town
but now it looks like the sea

as we descend
we pass broken religious iconography
and children's toys
and gun emplacements
and blackened clay sculptures
and things that we can't guess what they are
but they are all sacred
and we leave them behind
your military-grade kevlar Miu Miu gloves
bone white, get stained
with thick moss
and alkaline rain
and the blood of small bugs
as you slap them against your skin

we are *there* now
the thick welted scar of the sky is
a molten afterimage above us;

a flayed bronze streak too fast for the sun to fill

down here the walls of the break are featureless
buffed basalt black lidless smoothed
but the ground seethes thinly underfoot
numberless strands of spidery red;
every one a conduit
to the big mothers deep deep deep down in the
crust
{some fade as others flicker into being}

it is, i realise
{the glimmer of a smile under the mask}
like an ecology of vines
overrun, essential
tectonic filaments have burst
through the onyx floor
singing crystal spires that are
many sided
spidery helixes grow around the indents
where we have stepped
you can hear its speed o' light hiss
if you do not focus on it
this is
information hewing itself into geological shape
a diamond net like a tourniquet
a fizzing river like a coiling snake
your arm vibrates, harmonising

in tune

lämmergeiers roost in the pitch tunnels above
they wheel and caw just above our heads
yellow eyes
roll in their sockets

you plug something in

i think of the fox."

You called this *Titan Rose*.

What is here in this writing — you, my I that I no
longer know? Are you trying to get at me? What else do
you get at?

First, the names of some designers and a short-lived
eagerness for writing science-fiction. There is the
influence of Iain M. Banks, who your dad loved, in
particular *Feersum Endjinn,* I think. The lämmergeiers,
drug-glanding and subterranean computer servers give
that away. There is music, too: Scott Walker's croon.
This was not long before he died. There is time, of
course: possible aeons of time, deep time and geological

time, time that trips down the steps just as your two protagonists do, just as everything gets warped the closer they get to the bottom of the canyon. You are playing clumsily with sci-fi's genre conventions but pinning them into place with the clarity of a brand name, an artist or a song. More broadly there is the prose poem, or perhaps your first reckoning with the form — I'm not sure where that came from. What got into you? Anne Carson maybe, but I don't think you'd read *Autobiography of Red* for some years yet. Also: an absence of any capitalisation, a diffuse androgyny, one instance of sex without texture, detail or role delineation, a white fox, and the desire to change.

And me, I, my I? What have I been doing — now that you got at me successfully, or rather that finally I got at myself, shedding you? If you really want to get at I, I'll tell you all you need to know.

In the club the other weekend I was high and lost my glasses. I pawed through my purse under the long blood of the lights while my fingers spidered over everything, blindly. Eventually they closed around a small badge of embossed black leather with a slim zip, the colour of oil. Behind the zip was the cherry chapstick from Colorado and above me someone with PROPERTY OF JESUS tattooed across their back had just climbed onto the decks but through my other eye I watched deer climb down from the mountains to snooze on people's lawns. There were slim shelves of old coarse snow in the hills.

The chapstick had a smiling brown dog on the barrel and a rime of black gunk around the cap. I saw a gold lab throw himself down into the sluice at the edge of the CVS parking lot as we got out of the car while its owner yelled stop. The night before we'd lain in a hot spring halfway up the San Luis valley and felt the cloistered stars above, the ice, our own nudity. Under clear water the colour of pitch our pale limbs knocked against each other like porcelain. It was warm under the surface but the tips of our hair froze. We were completely unornamented. By which I mean there was nothing to mediate. It hadn't been like that for a long time.

That night you drove quietly through total darkness while decrepit Dollar General's the colour of banana medicine squatted on the haunches of the highway, leaking light. Between their sickly yellow glow and the sudden absence of the moon all the grisly mythology of the American West set in. A pickup followed too close behind us along a long dirt track and at that moment I understood why people want guns. Not why they have them, just what the feeling is.

In the morning there were deer out the window and I stole out of bed to watch the dawn come up in the cold. You were sleeping. I was used to seeing the horizon give out over the ocean but never at land alone. Calling this a valley seemed like a mistake. There were tiny black birds in the cottonwoods and a silvery geodesic dome out front and that's how you found me: staring at the mountains in the distance and under a quiet so total it kind of folded in on itself. That great big flattening. I want to say that you were wrapped in a duvet but I don't think that's true. That would mean that some heat had been carried between the sheets, that it was contained there; that such heat was enough to warm one person alone. I want to say that I know what I was thinking about but my whole body was skipping each hour like a tuning fork and somehow I pushed it all down.

I recount events this way and I don't know who it's for. Marlo says it's like running towards and away from yourself in opposite directions. And also that you can't have faith in something which you know exists. I say it's like taking a chisel to a glacier.

~

Much later, not long after the music had died and you read aloud about tracing lines in the dark while Rory made sounds at his desk, in the round, you and Francis went drinking. You went drinking to share writing, ostensibly, which you did and also drank. You clutched your starchy print outs and folded each poem four times to fit in the breast pocket of the red motorbike jacket Harry leant you over a decade ago and which you would never return. Together, you and Fran, you were kicked out of your old haunt at closing, and so sauntered down the street to a pub neither of you had been in before where the ceiling was emblazoned in a crypto-nationalist fresco: an enclave of solemn Templars loomed over the revellers derisively and you scattered your pages widely across a sticky brown table to say small, gentle things about a phrase; the way a line broke. You loved "inside me there is a punched clay well of a million, million terrible poems" and still do. Fran spoke about things dear to them, as they do: about Bernadette Mayer, data, (remember Tanoa saying "the data of water") about *Memory*; Fanny Howe intoning "be strong Bernadette" at Mayer's memorial in the East Village; Howe so weak that she had to be helped off the stage; Fran sobbing audibly at the back, and God the path to the toilets in the basement was just absolutely arcane; tiled mint green; two white wines and three whiskeys, each Templar stared on impassively; the whole place screaming hot and so busy, just steaming;

more whiskey and two more white wines and the grain and the grape and down into the labyrinthine toilets again, perhaps your last time then, because next you read a line you'd written back to yourself so silently while F went for a piss and then you read it and re-read it again until something started to slip your own gravity. It was cold and January. There was no ice. In your head always Anne Carson saying: "one notices different degrees of ice".[90]

That was it.

I don't know where you went after that. Maybe one day I'll find out. For now I like to think of you sitting on a style at the edge of a green field, or squatting on the stones deep down by the water, in thought. Always so pensive. Absorbed somewhere. But really no. I'll choose to think of you otherwise because this next one is real: as you were in that one photo, maybe the only photo — certainly the last — of you that I ever liked.

You were so hungover. Obliteratingly so. The kind of hangover that you never quite get back from. A digression scratched down somewhere, tallied up; a permanent, momentary trespass into a territory not quite of the living. You've propped yourself up against the low stone wall of an old mine complex at the edge of the Atlantic, all spun over with moss. Arsenic leaks slowly out of the cracks in the cliff far behind you, staining its face sickly turquoise, in streaks. The soil is a thick oxide red and the sky silver white grey all thin wash salt and whipping. Underneath: miles of obsolete tunnels stretch out tendrilous and deep, low, black and long under the sea. You managed to throw a stone through the gaps in the fence and down the slim opening into the old shaft. It made no sound for a long time. They mined tin and arsenic here. A year later the cab driver would explain that he started working down the pits at seventeen because it paid almost ten times better than any other work around, and because he had a girlfriend he hoped to marry. You were alone. In the photo at least. Alone with yourself as you were. That baggy silhouette always; ragged washed-out black metal hoodie and the big black jeans. There you are. So hungover. Your eyes closed. I was about to type *at peace* but I suppose I mean to say *defeated*. There is not an ounce of will left in you: you are leaving it behind.

It would make sense if this was the end. At the edge of the world like this, at the slip of the limit where it all started. So spent. But no. You picked yourself up and lugged your bones along with you and you walked back up that cliff edge to walk back into your own life, to struggle and hammer for as long as whatever was left in you would take to give out, and someone gave you an apple and honestly half the reason you even got up from that wall at all was because Ben extended his hand and held you; let you lean on his shoulder. It pains and scares me that you were a person who could push their whole life to a point of such wretched untenability. That it was easier, somehow, for you, you thought, to go along like that — spiralling for a decade, for fifteen years, than to finally give up the ghost. I try so hard to shy away from or to avoid slipping into the framing that in fact I am dead, or I was dead and now I am not, or really that you are dead and I am still alive but sometimes it truly does feel like that. The other day I bumped into a guy on the street who I haven't seen in six or seven years and immediately rippled with the absolute knowledge that the person he was trying to access was permanently and irretrievably gone.

Perhaps in time there will be a You that I can hold. A You I will be able to squeeze from coal and turn into a diamond. Something transparent that can be looked through. But you do not need to be perfect, neither do I, that was never what any of this was about. For now at least, in this epistolary exercise, you are necessarily You here, and I am I, as Me now, because She — and I've waited until now to speak about her — She is like an eclipse: you can't look at her directly without sufficient protection. Without the accreted words and these pages and all of it and the little black markings and the way they fill up the white space. They're the gauze that allows you to look at her without being blinded, which was the case for You too. She got to you, as I got to you, through language. She climbed through an aperture in language, through the slit in the sentence in the page that you read and re-read over and over in the pub while F went for a piss; which you watched to see if it moved or shook or simply folded back in on itself, or slipped off the page entirely, just as you watched yourself in the mirror hours later, after you got lost on the way home, to see if She, your body, whether it would buckle or shake or simply collapse back in on itself as it always would and yet it didn't, not this time, it was still. She was still. You looked at her and She looked at you and you saw yourself. And then She stepped in.

That's it.

Goodbye,

H x

One night last summer I touched a little sliver of God. Was up on the hill you know. By my house. Lying in the long grass and coiled tight under a cold screw of anguish. Could have drilled down into the sod. Lids clamped tight thrashing back and forth the sky black brown and the cold wind scolding me. Roooooohwwww went the trees. Told me the shape of ten years lost was a pit in the ground and I'd dug it. Accepted a contingency and cut my teeth on the limit. Tried to starve it out. And all that telescoping had made me half-mad you know like actually quite crazy for a little bit. Moon fat and off-white like a big fleck of puss. Then it stilled. Guts stopped hot screaming the trees wailing and just lay there. All quiet. Felt her nibble on my shoe first: she'd snuck up so silent like a splinter. Slow gnawing at the black sole, thin film, little blotches of white spit. Then sat with me. Curled up and went to sleep. We lay there together for a bit while the city kept up its whole thing — the evil lights in the distance, the river. Think I blacked out. She snapped me. I was pouring. Thought: Boundaries Are For Landlords and took two photos with the flash. Her legs all gathered underneath her like a dart. A real knife of a dog, or something. And the dandelions, the ribwort, lowly bowing beneath her ribs.

223

Before she left she circled me twice like something had died there. Then nicked a hole in the night and was gone.

s o   glean the last tin kering smirks of f   the frozen   eart h a nd   dis a llow   not hi n g

An earlier draft of *Shellac* was included in *Tissue Papers #1 - Making* ed. by Donna Marcus and Sam Moore, in May 2023. *Slagheap* was produced for Ⓐ DUDLEY Ⓔ and Jake Kent's collaborative exhibition *Demo Version Is Way Better* at Village Gallery, Leeds in March 2024. *Your Dress Says Easy Target* was originally published, untitled, in *Responses to Forbidden Colours (1988) by Felix Gonzales-Torres* for Pilot Press, November 2023.

[1] Kathy Acker, 'Seeing Gender' – in *Bodies of Work: Essays* (Serpents Tail, 1997) pp. 159

[2] Acker's last notebook, quoted by Chris Kraus in *After Kathy Acker: A Biography* (Penguin, 2018) pp. 15

[3] Clarice Lispector, *A Breath of Life (Pulsations)*, trans. Idra Novey / Johnny Lorenz (New Directions, 2012) pp. 65

[4] Fanny Howe, *London-rose | Beauty Will Save the World* (Divided Publishing, 2022) pp. 30

[5] Lucy Lippard, *Eva Hesse* (New York University Press, 1976) – this reference is found in the index, 'Notes to the Text' no. 5, pp. 215

[6] Susan Howe, *Debths* (New Directions, 2013) pp. 10

[7] Gerardo Madera, *Name, Thing, Thing: A Primer in Parallel Typographies*, (Printer Matter, Inc. 2018)

[8] Anne Michaels, *Infinite Gradiation* (House Sparrow Press, 2017) pp. 23

[9] Jack Spicer, 'Ballad of the Seven Passages' – in *After Lorca* (New York Review Books, 2021) pp. 14

[10] Edward Said's review of *Prisoner of Love* by Jean Genet, The Observer (Sunday 19th March 1989)

[11] Fanny Howe, *London-rose | Beauty Will Save the World* (Divided Publishing, 2022) pp. 33

[12] Samuel R. Delaney, *Heavenly Breakfast*, (Bamberger Books, 1997) pp. 103

[13] Hilton Als, 'Tristes Tropiques' in *White Girls* (McSweeney's, 2014) pp. 14

[14] Michael Holquist, prologue to *Rabelais and His World* by Mikhail Bakhtin (Indiana University Press, 2009) pp.15

[15] Each of the quotes in this section derive from Bakhtin, *Rabelais and His World*, Chapter 5: 'The Grotesque Image of the Body and its Sources' pp. 303-367

[16] J. M Cohen, introduction to *Gargantua and Pantagruel* by Francois Rabelais (Penguin Classics, 1955) pp. 17

[17] Fanny Howe, *Night Philosophy* (Divided Publishing, 2020) pp. 70

[18] Jenny Turner, *Literary Friction*, London Review of Books (Vol. 39 No. 20 · 19th October 2017 – accessed here: https://www.lrb.co.uk/the-paper/v39/n20/jenny-turner/literary-friction)

[19] Kraus quoted in interview with Matias Viegener, *The Life, Death, and Afterlife of Kathy Acker*, Los Angeles Review of Books (11th September 2017 – accessed here: https://lareviewofbooks.org/article/the-life-death-and-afterlife-of-kathy-acker)

[20] Sheila Heti, *Interview with Chris Kraus*, The Believer (September 1st, 2013 – accessed here: https://www.thebeliever.net/an-interview-with-chris-kraus/)

[21] Cynthia Cruz, *The Melancholia of Class: A Manifesto for the Working Class* (Repeater, 2021) pp. 15

[22] *ibid*. pp. 15

[23] Kathy Acker, 'Section from: Part III of Breaking Through Memories Into Desire' – letter sent to Alan Sondheim ca. February 24-28, 1974 in *Kathy Acker 1971-1975: Unpublished early writings* (éditions ismael, 2019) pp. 434

[24] Chris Kraus, *Aliens & Anorexia* (Semiotext(e) 2007) pp. 166

[25] *ibid*. pp. 103

[26] Elizabeth Hardwick, 'Simone Weil' in *The Collected Essays of Elizabeth Hardwick* (New York Review Books Classics, 2017) pp. 251

[27] Kraus, *Aliens* pp. 49

[28] *ibid*. pp. 51

[29] Simone Pétrement, *Simone Weil: A Life* (trans. Raymond Rosenthal, Pantheon Books, 1976) pp. 27

[30] Chris Kraus, *Posthumous* – review of *Simone Weil* by Palle Yourgrau, Los Angeles Review of Books (May 31st, 2011 – accessed here: https://lareviewofbooks.org/article/posthumous/)

[31] Francine du Plessix Gray, *Simone Weil* (Viking, 2001) pp. 20

[32] Kraus, *Aliens* pp. 51

[33] *ibid.* pp. 50

[34] Pétrement, *Simone Weil* pp. 420

[35] Hardwick, *The Collected Essays* pp. 250

[36] Pétrement, *Simone Weil* pp. 7

[37] *ibid.* pp. 11

[38] Kraus, *Aliens* pp. 49

[39] Lucy Lippard, *Eva Hesse* (New York University Press, 1976) pp. 6

[40] *ibid.* pp. 6

[41] *ibid.* pp. 5

[42] Kraus, *Aliens* pp. 49

[43] Hardwick, *Collected Essays* pp. 252

[44] Pétrement, *Simone Weil* pp. 537

[45] Peggy Phelan, *Mourning Sex: Performing Public Memories* (Routledge, 1997) pp. 2

[46] Kraus, *Aliens* pp. 48

[47] Howe, *Night Philosophy* pp. 90

[48] Kraus, *Aliens* pp. 48

[49] *ibid.* pp. 49

[50] Hardwick, *The Collected Essays* pp. 257

[51] Pétrement, *Simone Weil* pp. 420

[52] Simone Weil, *Gravity and Grace* (Routledge Classics, 2002) pp. 100

[53] Kraus, *Aliens* pp. 182

[54] Pétrement, *Simone Weil* pp. 421

[55] Simone Weil, 'The Iliad or, The Poem of Force' – in *Politics*, November 1945, pp. 322

[56] *ibid.* pp. 321

[57] *ibid.* pp. 321

[58] Susan Howe, 'Arisbe' – in *The Quarry* (New Directions Press, 2015) pp. 83

[59] Pétrement, *Simone Weil* pp. 271

[60] Kraus, quoting Simone's *Gravity and Grace,* in *Aliens,* pp. 50

[61] Anne Carson, 'Decreation: How Women Like Sappho, Marguerite Porete and Simone Weil Tell God' – in *Decreation* (Jonathan Cape, 2006) pp. 167

[62] Simone Weil, *Gravity and Grace* (University of Nebraska Press, 1997) pp. 71

[63] Carson, *Decreation* pp. 69

[64] Weil, *Gravity and Grace* (Nebraska Press) pp. 88

[65] *Wasted: A Memoir of Anorexia and Bulimia,* Marya Hornbacher (Harper Perennial, 1999) pp. 134

[66] Kraus, quoting Richard Rees – in *Aliens* pp. 142

[67] *ibid.* pp. 51

[68] This phrase is from the blurb of *Aliens,* Semiotext(e) ed.

[69] Hilton Als, 'Tristes Tropiques' in *White Girls* (McSweeney's, 2014) pp. 88

[70] Kraus, *Aliens* pp.163

[71] *ibid.* pp. 165

[72] *ibid.* pp. 137

[73] *ibid.* pp. 160

[74] *ibid.* pp. 160

[75] *ibid.* pp. 162

[76] *ibid.* pp. 50

[77] *ibid.* pp. 49

[78] *ibid.* pp. 133

[79] *ibid.* pp. 138

[80] *ibid.* pp. 163

[81] *ibid.* pp. 167

[82] *ibid.* pp. 167

[83] Hornbacher, *Wasted* pp. 275

[84] *ibid.* pp. 279

[85] Kraus, *Aliens* pp. 182

[86] *ibid.* pp. 51

[87] *ibid.* pp. 161